SEEKING FIRST THE KINGDOM

30 Meditations on How to Love God with All Your Heart, Soul, Mind, and Strength

Fr. John Bartunek, L.C., S.Th.D.

Published by Ministry23, LLC
2401 Harnish Dr., Suite 100
Algonquin, Illinois 60102
ministry23.com

Imprimi Potest, Luis Garza, LC, JDC
Nihil Obstat, Eric R. Barr, STL
Imprimatur, +Most Reverend David J. Malloy, DD, JCL, STD

Cover design: Coronation Media
coronationmedia.com

ISBN 978-0-9916038-0-0
Library of Congress Control Number: 2014937369

Printed in the United States of America
5 4 3 2

TABLE OF CONTENTS

Part V: Loving God with All My Strength

Part VI: Getting Practical

Introduction

THIS BOOK IS mainly for those who are newly intrigued by Jesus Christ and find themselves wanting to follow him more closely. That desire is the most precious gift God can give to a human heart, because friendship with Jesus Christ is the only path to lasting fulfillment.

But if you feel that desire deeply—if you truly burn with a longing to know Jesus more and more clearly, to love him more and more dearly, and to follow him more and more nearly (to borrow three phrases from a medieval prayer by St. Richard of Chichester)—you will run up against obstacles and roadblocks every step of the way. These obstacles can easily drain that precious desire to seek greater intimacy with God. They can disorient, discourage, and jade even the most well-intentioned Christians. And that can happen at any point in the spiritual journey: the beginning, the middle, or the end. So this book is not only for those just starting. It's also for those who would like some fresh encouragement and some motivating reminders along the way.

Spiritual Integration

One sure way to keep our holy desires strong and vibrant, in spite of roadblocks, is to understand the concept of spiritual integration: bringing every dimension of our being and personality into play in our relationship with God.

Friendship with Christ is a unique friendship, because Jesus is a unique friend. He is not *only* a loyal and loving companion; he is *also* the Lord—Creator and Redeemer of the human race, uniquely worthy of worship and obedience. Friendship with Christ grows, therefore, by allowing Christ's companionship and lordship to touch and transform every sector of our existence: all our internal powers, which subsequently manifest themselves in all our external activities. This extension of Christ's influence to every corner of our life is the essence of spiritual integration; we gradually integrate, more and more deeply, every facet of our person and experience into our friendship with Jesus Christ. We learn to live more and more *in* Jesus, and he comes to live more and more *in* us. This is the amazing journey toward spiritual maturity.

Life in Christ

This mysterious connection between Christ and the Christian constitutes one of the main themes of the New Testament. St. Paul especially refers to the phrase "in Christ" over and over again. Everything changes for the person who has come to share in Christ's life:

> *So whoever is in Christ is a new creation: the old things have passed away; behold, new things have come.* (2 Corinthians 5:17)

And Jesus himself becomes the life of the one who welcomes him through faith:

> *I have been crucified with Christ; yet I live, no longer I, but Christ lives in me; insofar as I now live in the flesh, I live by faith in the Son of God who has loved me and given himself up for me.* (Galatians 2:19–20)

Normal friendship entails an intimate sharing between two people. As Aristotle is attributed with saying, friendship is "a single soul dwelling in two bodies." But when one of those two souls is infinite and perfect, then intimate sharing is not enough. In this case, the lesser of the two must also allow himself to be transformed and elevated by the greater. This is the case with a Christian and Christ. We must walk with Jesus through life, but we also must humbly and lovingly conform ourselves to Christ (this is what it means to "follow" Jesus Christ) in order to allow this grace-filled friendship to reach maturity. Only thus can we enter fully into Christ's kingdom—the one kingdom where our longings for an eternally meaningful life can be fulfilled.

Guided by the Holy Spirit

We are not alone in our efforts to conform to Christ. Jesus accompanies us, and actually enables us, every step of the way, especially through the presence and action of the Holy Spirit. St. John Paul II, whose words will accompany you along your journey through these thirty meditations, repeated that essential truth over and over again. For example:

> *Following Christ is not an outward imitation, since it touches man at the very depths of his being. Being a follower of Christ means becoming conformed to him who became a servant even to giving himself on the cross. Christ dwells by faith in the heart of the believer, and thus the disciple is conformed to the Lord. This is the effect of grace, of the active presence of the Holy Spirit in us.*[1]

Requiring Our Free Cooperation

And yet, Jesus refuses to do all the work himself. He includes us in the project, sharing the work with us. We have to choose, freely and repeatedly, to be faithful to the friendship. Otherwise, it would not be a friendship at all—we would just be pre-programmed Christian robots. But that's not what we were created for. We were created in God's image, to give glory to him by freely living in communion with him, in whom alone we find our lasting happiness.

And so, in this Christian adventure, in this journey toward spiritual maturity, we have a part to play. We are co-protagonists in the process of integrating every facet of our existence into our friendship with Jesus. We are co-conquerors in the battle to bring every sector of our personality and experience and activity under the infinitely wise and sure rule of Christ the Lord.

How do we do our part? How do we cooperate with Jesus to Christianize every single corner of our lives? Jesus sums up the answer with a liberating simplicity:

1 John Paul II, *Veritatis Splendor,* 21.

> *But seek first the kingdom (of God) and his righteousness, and all these things will be given you besides.* (Matthew 6:33)

Seeking God's kingdom first, seeking to allow Christ the Eternal King to rule and guide our lives in accordance with his wisdom, goodness, and love, seeking to abide by the Lord's life-giving standards in all that we think, say, and do—this is every Christian's primary task. It is the basic commitment that we make when we fall in love with God and give our hearts to him. Following through on that commitment is how we do our part in allowing God's grace free rein to order and energize our lives on earth, and to bring us to the fullness of eternal life in heaven.

Loving with Everything We've Got

Seeking something involves knowing about it, wanting it, and going out to take possession of it. These three activities correspond to the three basic powers of the human soul: the *mind*, which knows and understands; the *emotions*, which feel attraction and repulsion; and the *will*, by which one makes decisions and takes action.

And so, in essence, seeking God's kingdom means seeking to let Jesus, the everlasting King, rule our minds with his infinite truth, our feelings with his endless beauty, and our decisions with his overflowing goodness. This is how our friendship with Christ matures. This is how we integrate our entire lives into his unique and life-giving friendship. This is how we allow God to transform and bring to full spiritual maturity our minds, our emotions, and our wills—our whole selves, every corner of our lives.

An Ongoing Adventure

The process of integration takes a lifetime, because we are always changing and growing, and because God himself, the one we are seeking, is infinite. Seeking first the kingdom, then, is not something that we can check off our to-do list once and for all. But the more intentionally and intelligently we engage in it, the more quickly and fully God's grace will extend the Lord's rule in our lives and move us further along the path of spiritual maturity.

These initial reflections on what it means to "seek first the kingdom of God" point toward Christ's own instructions about how to do just that. When he was asked to identify the first and greatest commandment, the path to spiritual maturity, he answered by saying:

> *The first is: "Hear, O Israel! The Lord our God is Lord alone! You shall love the Lord your God with all your heart, with all your soul, with all your mind, and with all your strength." The second is this: "You shall love your neighbor as yourself." There is no other commandment greater than these.* (Mark 12:29–31)

By using the verb *love*, Jesus centers the human vocation to holiness and happiness not simply on personal achievements, but rather on a relationship—on a personal relationship of intimate and mutual self-giving with God, which happens through friendship with Jesus.

Then, by specifying "heart, soul, mind, and strength," Jesus points out the importance of integrating our whole personality—every facet of our humanity—into our friendship with God. In this book we will explore each one of those four areas individually, even though in real life they always go together; each one influences and affects all the others.

Finally, by emphasizing that we are to love God with *all* our "heart, soul, mind, and strength," Jesus indicates the dynamism of this lifetime adventure; it has no limit—we can always deepen our intimacy with God, expand our spiritual integration, and discover new depths of meaning and fulfillment.

This book is an extended reflection on the wealth of wisdom that God has poured into that greatest of all commandments. It unpacks and explores the many implications of what it means to seek first Christ's kingdom by loving "the Lord your God with all your heart, with all your soul, with all your mind, and with all your strength." The second greatest commandment, "You shall love your neighbor as yourself," since it is so closely related to the first, also deserves to be unpacked and explored. But that task is important and large enough to deserve its own treatment; it will be the task of a separate book of meditations.

Using This Book

The thirty short chapters of this book provide explanations and reflections that can help you seek Christ's kingdom and love him with everything you've got, intentionally and intelligently. They are meant to be used for personal meditation or spiritual reading and also for group study and discussion. Praying through one chapter a day can give you a month-long spiritual retreat. The abundant biblical quotations are presented in red in order to make prayer and meditation on God's sacred Word easier, if you use the book in this way .

Working through one chapter a week together with a group of friends can provide a richly rewarding path of Christ-centered fellowship. The questions for reflection at the end of each chapter can serve either as aids for personal reflection and prayer or as helps to spark invigorating small-group interaction. Each chapter's concluding prayer, drawn from various sources that make up the vast, two-thousand-year-old treasury of Christian spirituality, can be prayed individually or as a group. The introductory quotations from St. John Paul II are meant to link the themes of each chapter to the Church's ongoing mission of renewed evangelization, which was so dear to the heart of the pope who led the Christian family across the threshold of the third millennium.

However you choose to take advantage of this resource, if you are truly seeking first the kingdom, you can't go wrong. After all, the Lord himself made the solemn promise: "Seek, and you will find" (Matthew 7:7, RSV).

PART I
God's Part and My Part

When a large crowd gathered, with people from one town after another journeying to him, [Jesus] spoke in a parable. "A sower went out to sow his seed. And as he sowed, some seed fell on the path and was trampled, and the birds of the sky ate it up. Some seed fell on rocky ground, and when it grew, it withered for lack of moisture. Some seed fell among thorns, and the thorns grew with it and choked it. And some seed fell on good soil, and when it grew, it produced fruit a hundredfold."

After saying this, he called out, "Whoever has ears to hear ought to hear.... This is the meaning of the parable. The seed is the word of God. Those on the path are the ones who have heard, but the devil comes and takes away the word from their hearts that they may not believe and be saved. Those on rocky ground are the ones who, when they hear, receive the word with joy, but they have no root; they believe only for a time and fall away in time of trial. As for the seed that fell among thorns, they are the ones who have heard, but as they go along, they are choked by the anxieties and riches and pleasures of life, and they fail to produce mature fruit. But as for the seed that fell on rich soil, they are the ones who, when they have heard the word, embrace it with a generous and good heart, and bear fruit through perseverance." (Luke 8:4–8, 11–15)

Chapter 1
How Much Is Up to Me?

We now need to profit from the grace received, by putting it into practice in resolutions and guidelines for action.
—St. John Paul II, *Novo Millennio Ineunte, 3*

JESUS SEEMS TO contradict himself. On the one hand, he tells us that "apart from me you can do nothing" (John 15:5, RSV). He is the vine, he explains in the same passage, and we are only branches, completely dependent on the flow of sap and life that comes to us through the vine. The word used for *nothing* in the Greek, in fact, is the simple, total negative—nothing at all, absolute zero.

Yet on the other hand, Jesus looks us in the eye and implores us, "Strive to enter by the narrow door; for many, I tell you, will seek to enter and will not be able" (Luke 13:24, RSV). Here he begs us to put all our effort into following him, obeying him, seeking him. The Greek word for *strive* connotes struggle, fight, and the kind of intensity that amazes us when we watch, riveted, as Olympic athletes battle for the gold.

What is going on here? How can we reconcile our Lord's injunction that we are absolutely helpless and dependent in the spiritual life with his command to fight to the death, as it were, in order to achieve spiritual maturity and salvation?

St. Paul to the Rescue?

What a relief it would be if St. Paul were to resolve the dilemma for us! But, this time anyway, he comes up short. He too, it seems, contradicts himself. In defending his apostolic credentials, he points out to the Christians in Corinth that "by the grace of God I am what I am, and his grace to me has not been ineffective. Indeed, I have toiled harder than all of them; not I, however, but the grace of God with me" (1 Corinthians 15:10).

Paul attributes all that he is and all that he has accomplished as a follower of Jesus to "the grace of God." But in the same breath, he claims to have contributed to his Christian greatness by having "toiled harder" than anybody else. The Greek word used for *toil* connotes wearisome, backbreaking exertion. Etymologically, it harkens back to a term associated with the demanding, harsh, and unrelenting work of an agricultural laborer before the advent of mechanized farm equipment. That's the kind of contribution St. Paul feels that he has made to his Christian mission, even while he affirms that God's grace is the sole source of all the good fruits his mission has borne.

We can see no light at the end of this tunnel. We are stuck with the paradox: Our Christian life depends entirely on God's grace, yet it also depends on our human efforts in order to make that grace bear fruit. It is a partnership.

The theologian-pope, Benedict XVI, affirmed this paradox without trying to explain it away when commenting on our Lord's parables about seeds:[1]

> *Every Christian, then, knows well that he must do all that he can, but that the final result depends on God: this knowledge sustains him in daily toil, especially in difficult situations.*

The Holy Father went on to quote the cavalier-turned-mystic, St. Ignatius of Loyola, to drive the point home:

> *Act as if everything depended on you, knowing that in reality everything depends on God.*

1 Benedict XVI, Angelus, June 18, 2012.

The Right Proportion

Here we have one of the many binary star systems, spiritually speaking, in the galaxy of the Gospels.

A binary star system happens when two stars share a common center of mass. In such a situation, their orbits are perfectly harmonized and inextricably interdependent. As one moves, the other moves. As one turns, the other turns. They seem to pull against each other, and yet the tension between them is actually the source of their dynamism. Likewise, in our growth toward spiritual maturity, the mysterious partnership between God's action and our action creates a healthy kind of tension from which spiritual dynamism flows.

Each binary star system consists of a brighter star (the primary star) and a dimmer star (the companion star). In our pursuit of intimacy with God—of the spiritual maturity that alone will yield the lasting fulfillment we are created for—God's grace is the primary star, and our effort is the companion star. God's grace is primary, 99 percent. Our striving is secondary, 1 percent. And yet, both are necessary; without the 1 percent, the job will not be done.

To switch analogies, think of cooking. The ingredients for a plate of primavera pasta come from myriad suppliers: the farmers who grow and harvest the wheat and the vegetables, the olive oil and the tomatoes (not to mention the God-given natural forces that give and sustain the lives of those plants); the transportation companies that bring those products to food-processing plants; the food-processing plants themselves; more transportation companies to put the goods in the grocery store; the grocery store team that preserves and arranges and sells.... By the time those ingredients are lined up on the kitchen counter and ready to be prepped and cooked, hundreds if not thousands of people have already contributed to the meal. That's like the 99 percent. And yet, unless someone chops, simmers, boils, and stirs, the meal will never make it to the table. That's like the 1 percent.

True Partners

St. Augustine, the great bishop from North Africa who helped the Church survive the cataclysmic fall of the western Roman Empire early on in Christian history, expressed this truth cleverly when he wrote: "God created us without us: but he did not will to save us without us."[2] God created us to live in a relationship with him, not to be robots. So, even though we are entirely dependent on him for our existence and our spiritual growth, he chooses to limit his omnipotence, in a sense, in order to leave us room to become true partners in salvation history.

S

Questions for Personal Reflection or Group Discussion

1. What idea in this chapter struck you most and why?

2. In what ways have you personally experienced this paradox of Christianity, this binary star system of God's grace and your effort?

3. Explain in your own words why God chooses to make the fruitfulness of his grace in your life depend so much on your collaboration.

4. What will you do today to keep yourself in better harmony with God, the "primary star" of your life?

    - I will say a short prayer of thanksgiving before each meal.
    - I will write a "note to God" thanking him for a specific blessing.
    - (Write your own resolution) I will_________________________.

Concluding Prayer

O God, strength of those who hope in you,
graciously hear our pleas,
and, since without you mortal frailty can do nothing,
grant us always the help of your grace,
that in following your commands we may please you by our resolve and our deeds.
—Roman Missal, Collect for the Eleventh Sunday in Ordinary Time

2 St. Augustine, *Sermo* 169,11,13:PL 38, 923.

Chapter 2
God Is Faithful

Christianity is grace, it is the wonder of a God who is not satisfied with creating the world and man, but puts himself on the same level as the creature he has made, and after speaking on various occasions and in different ways through his prophets, "in these last days…has spoken to us by a Son" (Hebrews 1:1–2).

—St. John Paul II, *Novo Millennio Ineunte,* 3

GOD'S GRACE IS never lacking. His 99 percent is always available. He never fails us. He never forgets about us. He never goes on vacation leaving us to fend for ourselves for a while. No—"God is faithful," St. Paul reminds us (1 Corinthians 1:9). Just as he took the initiative to create and redeem us, beginning in us the "good work" of holiness, so he "will bring it to completion at the day of Christ Jesus" (Philippians 1:6). The *Catechism of the Catholic Church* reminds us of this in its very first paragraph:

> *For this reason, at every time and in every place, God draws close to man. He calls man to seek him, to know him, to love him with all his strength. (CCC, 1)*

God's grace, his action, his part, is never lacking. It reaches out to us and surrounds us and sustains us at every time and in every place, like the very atmosphere we breathe.

This is the bottom line in our friendship with Christ. This is the starting line and the finishing line. Jesus, his trustworthiness, his faithfulness, his absolute dependability and unlimited loyalty—this is the "Alpha and the Omega, the first and the last, the beginning and the end" (Revelation 22:13, RSV).

A Message from the Cross

This was one of the reasons that God chose to save us through the betrayal, humiliation, torture, crucifixion, and death of his only-begotten Son. Saving us that way shows, once and for all, that nothing we do can cause God to give up on us. He stayed faithful to us, loving and forgiving us, throughout the horrible injustices and crimes that we committed against him during Christ's passion and death. And after all that, he still loves us and reaches out to us and offers us his grace. Because of that, we have absolute assurance of his undying faithfulness.

St. Paul understood this as well as anyone, and better than most. He put it like this in his letter to the Christians in Rome:

> *What then shall we say to this? If God is for us, who can be against us? He who did not spare his own Son but handed him over for us all, how will he not also give us everything else along with him? (Romans 8:31–32)*

In his encyclical letter *Lumen Fidei,* Pope Francis gave this fundamental truth brilliant expression. He wrote (emphasis added):

> *The history of Jesus is the complete manifestation of* God's reliability.... *The clearest proof of the reliability of Christ's love is to be found in his dying for our sake. If laying down one's life for one's friends is the greatest proof of love (cf. John 15:13), Jesus offered his own life for all, even for his enemies, to transform their hearts. This explains why the evangelists could see the hour of Christ's crucifixion as the culmination of the gaze of faith;* in that hour the depth and breadth of God's love shone forth.[1]

Learning to Trust

It's easy to say but hard to live; it's hard to trust that God will always be do-

1 Pope Francis, *Lumen Fidei,* 15–16.

ing his part, the 99 percent, even when we waver or get sloppy in doing our 1 percent.

Our modern, post-Christian culture steadily feeds us the lie that if we just work a little bit harder, or a little bit smarter, we can create heaven on earth; we can perfect ourselves. We tend to believe the lie, because even in the safest of harbors, in the bosom of our family when we're growing up, we discover that human approval and affection can (and sometimes even *must*) be earned. And so this lie seeps into our relationship with God. We feel as if we need to make ourselves worthy of God's grace; he will only do his part, we mistakenly tell ourselves, if we do our part really, really well.

God knows how hard it is for us to trust him, and he is always looking for ways to help us out. As a result, the story of salvation that unfolds in the pages of the Bible comes back to the truth of God's utter reliability over and over again, like a refrain. God manifests his faithfulness to his people all the way from the very beginning, through the experiences of Abraham, Moses, all the kings and prophets of the Old Testament, and all the apostles and saints of the New Testament. Maybe the Blessed Virgin Mary expressed it best when she simply proclaimed: "His mercy is from age to age" (Luke 1:50, RSV).

Images that Inspire Confidence

The prayer book of the Old Testament (and of the Church), the Psalms, draws on images from the natural world to dispel the hesitancy of our fallen nature and emblazon confidence in God on our hearts. Read Psalm 36:5–6, for example:

> *LORD, your mercy reaches to heaven;*
> *your fidelity, to the clouds.*
> *Your justice is like the highest mountains;*
> *your judgments, like the mighty deep.*

The psalmist compares the immeasurable qualities of God to some of the most evocative scenes of the created world. The vast expanse of the sky, the atmosphere that surrounds and upholds us every moment, whether or not we are aware of it, is a pale reflection of the Lord's "mercy and faithfulness."

Is there a limit to the sky, to the heavens? Not one that we can see or experience. Just so, God's forgiveness, goodness, and love have no limits.

The solidity, the firmness, the unflagging and monumentally dependable presence of the mountains show forth to the inspired psalmist the absolute firmness of God's justice—a Hebrew word connoting truth and faithfulness, utter reliability.

The vast and mysterious power and motion of the sea, so mesmerizing, inviting, and awe-inspiring, are for the psalmist a glimpse of the untiring wisdom of God—his judgments, his will, his attentive and intimate governance of all things.

This is our God. This is the Lord who is always doing his part. This is the bedrock of our faith and the steady assurance that allows us to stumble along joyfully at his side as we make a decent effort to do our part. It starts with him. It always starts with him.

S

Questions for Personal Reflection or Group Discussion

1. What idea in this chapter struck you most and why?

2. When have you experienced personally God's amazing faithfulness? (Remember, consider, and give thanks.)

3. What are some of the factors in your life that keep you from trusting God more fully?

4. Confidence in God can show itself in many different ways throughout the ups and downs of your daily life. It can soften the blows of disappointment or loss, since you know that God loves to work wonders out of weakness. It can fill you with courage to do the right thing, what you know is truly right, even when peer pressure is violently pulling you in the wrong direction, because you know that God's way is always the better way. It can free you to rejoice in the successes of other people, instead of resenting them, because you know that God's love for you doesn't depend on winning competitions. What will you do today to express your confidence in God?

- I will humbly accept my human limitations by saying "no" to good opportunities or invitations that would require me to overcommit.
- I will simply say a prayer for someone who is struggling and wants to unreasonably draw me into their tangled situation, instead of thinking that it's up to me to solve everyone's problems.
- I will visit the grave of a loved one and surrender that person into God's care once and for all, letting go—through prayer—of the resentment or fear that still accompanies my feelings of loss.
- (Write your own resolution) I will______________________________

Concluding Prayer

We give you praise, Father most holy, for you are great and you have fashioned all your works in wisdom and in love.
You formed man in your own image and entrusted the whole world to his care, so that in serving you alone, the Creator, he might have dominion over all creatures.
And when through disobedience he had lost your friendship, you did not abandon him to the domain of death.
For you came in mercy to the aid of all, so that those who seek might find you.

—Roman Missal, from Eucharistic Prayer IV

Chapter 3
The Spiritual Combat

St. Paul's words (especially in the Letters to the Romans and Galatians) enable us to know and feel vividly the strength of the tension and struggle going on in man between openness to the action of the Holy Spirit and resistance and opposition to him...
—St. John Paul II, *Dominum et Vivificantem,* 55

THE DEVIL, OUR ancient enemy, really exists. Jesus talked about him a lot. The *Catechism* emphasizes the reality of this fallen angel, who is interested in interfering with the adventure of love we are called to live:

> *Evil is not an abstraction, but refers to a person, Satan, the Evil One, the angel who opposes God. The devil is the one who 'throws himself across' God's plan and his work of salvation accomplished in Christ. (CCC, 2851)*

And the devil knows the truth that we examined in the last chapter, that God is faithful, that divine grace will never fail us. The devil knows that he cannot obstruct the flow of God's grace at its source. He can, however, clog up the channels by which we normally receive that grace. He can confuse and distract the minds and hearts to which God's grace is directed, turning us into bad receivers, bad cooperators, irresponsible partners. This is his strategy.

Enemies of Our Spiritual Growth

And our ancient enemy has powerful allies: the fallen world (all the corrupting and wounding influences that come from the proliferation of sin in human society and culture) and our fallen human nature (our own internal divisions and insecurities that make us vulnerable to temptation). Because of these, we have built-in tendencies that continually nudge us away from God's grace and disturb the spiritual docility needed for that grace to be fruitful in our lives. St. John refers to these negative influences when he warns the early Christians:

> *Do not love the world or the things of the world. If anyone loves the world, the love of the Father is not in him. For all that is in the world, sensual lust, enticement for the eyes, and a pretentious life, is not from the Father but is from the world." (1 John 2:15–16)*

The fallen world in which we live—though good in its essence because it was created by God—can be a snare for us fallen human beings. This is why the Church has never ceased to remind us that the spiritual life is, at least in part, also a spiritual combat:

> *Therefore man is split within himself. As a result, all of human life, whether individual or collective, shows itself to be a dramatic struggle between good and evil, between light and darkness... The whole of man's history has been the story of dour combat with the powers of evil, stretching, so our Lord tells us, from the very dawn of history until the last day. Finding himself in the midst of the battlefield man has to struggle to do what is right, and it is at great cost to himself, aided by God's grace, that he succeeds in achieving his own inner integrity.*[2]

An Interior Battle

This spiritual combat doesn't happen with guns and swords and tanks and missiles. It takes place much more subtly, often invisibly, in the intimate arena of human freedom. It has to do with our daily choices, whether large or small. It has to do with how we use the gift of free will that we have received.

2 Second Vatican Council, *Gaudium et Spes,* 13, 27.

God, as well as our better self, wants us to use that freedom to choose, step after step, the path of union and friendship with Christ, the path of abundant life, the path of obedience to his wise and loving plan for the human family: "I came so that they might have life and have it more abundantly. I am the good shepherd" (John 10:10–11).

Our enemy and our fallen nature, on the other hand, want us to use our free will in order to choose a different path, a path strewn with false promises (that we can somehow be fulfilled without God, for instance) and false ideas about God and ourselves (we are unloveable, God is untrustworthy, holiness is beyond our reach, it's not worth trying anymore, etc.).

This path often appears to offer easier and quicker access to happiness, but in fact it leads to interior disintegration and emptiness, because the devil is "a murderer…a liar and the father of lies" (John 8:44, RSV) and because sin always has evil consequences: "For the wages of sin is death" (Romans 6:23, RSV).

Spiritual combat is the ongoing battle between these contrary forces: Which will we choose to follow? St. Peter sums it up vividly in his first letter. First, he points out our need to be watchful:

> *Be sober and vigilant. Your opponent the devil is prowling around like a roaring lion looking for [someone] to devour. Resist him, steadfast in faith…*

And then he reminds us that our vigilance should never be harsh and desperate, but calm and joyful, even when it's hard, because God is with us:

> *The God of all grace who called you to his eternal glory through Christ [Jesus] will himself restore, confirm, strengthen, and establish you after you have suffered a little. (1 Peter 5:8–10)*

Sometimes our choices are stark and obvious, as when the Israelites abandoned God in the wilderness by worshipping the golden calf, or when David laid his life on the line by going out to face Goliath.

Yet, although some individual choices may be stark, the process by which we make those choices is complex. We arrive at big-decision moments with a predisposition for self-giving or self-centeredness, for docility or resistance to God's action in our lives. The gradual formation of that predisposition is the real, day-to-day spiritual battleground. The predisposition is built up from many little, seemingly insignificant choices that gradually fill in our spiritual profile: choices about how we spend our time; whom we befriend; what we say and how we say it; and how we react to unforeseen opportunities, difficulties, or temptations.

Through the exercise of our free will in the little choices we make, we are either furthering Christ's kingdom and growing in spiritual maturity, or we are inhibiting that kingdom and stunting our spiritual growth. As Jesus put it:

> *The person who is trustworthy in very small matters is also trustworthy in great ones; and the person who is dishonest in very small matters is also dishonest in great ones.* (Luke 16:10)

Small Battles Prepare Us for Bigger Battles

Jesus illustrated the relationship between the many small choices that prepare us for bigger decisions by using a construction image. He likened the spiritual life to the construction of a house. We build gradually, through choices in or out of harmony with his wisdom. Then comes a storm, a stark choice, a big decision, a decisive temptation. Our response to the storm is conditioned by all the small choices that went into building up our spiritual edifice:

> *Everyone who listens to these words of mine and acts on them will be like a wise man who built his house on rock. The rain fell, the floods came, and the winds blew and buffeted the house. But it did not collapse; it had been set solidly on rock. And everyone who listens to these words of mine but does not act on them will be like a fool who built his house on sand. The rain fell, the floods came, and the winds blew and buffeted the house. And it collapsed and was completely ruined.* (Matthew 7:24–27)

Spiritual Responsibility

Before he became bishop and then pope, St. John Paul II was known for his wise advice in the confessional. But he was also known for the delicate respect he showed to those who came to confession. After helping them sort through their confusion and their trouble, and after identifying some possible next steps, he would always say, "But now it is up to you; you must choose."

This is the battlefield of the spiritual combat: the intimate and mysterious arena of human freedom. Every day we enter that arena anew. There, through our decisions, we make ourselves more into one of two kinds of people—either the kind of person who stays faithful to what is true, good, and beautiful, or the kind of person who prefers an easier path, namely, the wide gate and the broad road that lead to destruction (see Matthew 7:13).

S

Questions for Personal Reflection or Group Discussion

1. What idea in this chapter struck you most and why?

2. How aware are you of your interior freedom, your God-given capacity to choose how you will act and react?

3. How does the reality of spiritual combat make you feel: excited, frightened, confused, humble? How do you think God wants this truth to make you feel?

4. Victor Frankl was a Jewish psychologist sent to a concentration camp in Nazi Germany. His experience of surviving the camp led him to develop a new school of psychology based on what he termed "logotherapy."[3] One of his key principles was: "Everything can be taken from a man but one thing: the last of the human freedoms—to choose one's attitude in any given set of circumstances, to choose one's own way." What will you do today to exercise more consciously this great gift of interior freedom?

    - I will say a prayer instead of retaliating when I feel attacked or misunderstood.
    - I will say no to my usual tendency to procrastinate regarding important things.

3 Victor Frankl, *Man's Search for Meaning* (Boston: Beacon Press, 2006).

- I will give myself some silence today, a few minutes to simply let my interior settle down and listen to what God may be saying to my heart.
- (Write your own resolution) ________________________________.

Concluding Prayer

Grant, O Lord, that we may begin with holy fasting
this campaign of Christian service,
so that, as we take up battle against spiritual evils,
we may be armed with weapons of self-restraint.

—Roman Missal, Collect from the Mass for Ash Wednesday

Chapter 4
Good Soil

Baptism is the sign that God has joined us on our journey, that he makes our existence more beautiful, and that he transforms our history into a history of holiness.
—St. John Paul II, World Youth Day Vigil, 1997

OUR LORD FREQUENTLY described his kingdom, the growth of his lordship in each heart and in the world, by comparing it to plants. The mustard seed (see Matthew 13:31), the farmer's field (see Matthew 13:24), the sower who sowed seed on various types of soil (see Luke 8:1-15)—all these images illustrate the essential partnership at the heart of our Christian journey.

The seed has an intrinsic power to grow and bear fruit. That power comes directly from God, not from anything the farmer can do. But the power to grow is only released under proper conditions: good soil, water, sunlight. Creating and maintaining the proper conditions for growth is the farmer's job. And it's a hard job. Lots of work is involved. But even if he did all that work extremely well, it would have no result without the God-given life inside the seed.

Which is more essential to a healthy crop, the seed or the soil? Neither. Both are equally essential. So it is with our growth in holiness. God's grace is the seed of new spiritual life planted in our souls through faith and baptism, the potential to become a saint, a unique reflection of God's infinite beauty, the glorious truth about God and ourselves in God's eyes. The soil is our part, our cooperation with and response to God, the healthy or unhealthy exercise of our freedom in the midst of the spiritual combat.

Our efforts—our choices and decisions—can provide and maintain healthy soil for the seed of God's grace to take root and flourish. Our lack of effort or misguided efforts can harden that soil or otherwise corrupt it, so that the seed of the kingdom is stolen, choked, or its growth truncated.

Seasons of Growth

Myriad practical lessons flow from this concept of spiritual growth. First of all, patience. Have you ever seen a farmer standing in his fields, yelling at his crops to grow faster? That would be absurd. Yet isn't that exactly what we do when we become frustrated with our slow spiritual progress, or the slow spiritual progress of others?

Then there is the lesson of rhythm. Spiritual growth goes through seasons. Plants need to grow to maturity before they bear fruit. Likewise, we need time in our Christian journey to get to the point where we can really bear abundant spiritual fruit. We need Nazareth seasons—seasons of quiet, ordinary, and undramatic activity and experience, when we are being prepared for the mission.

Even when plants are mature, they have periods when they are seemingly dry and dormant, under attack, so to speak, by harsh conditions: the wintry months. So too, in the spiritual life, we experience wintry seasons, when all we find in our souls is dryness, darkness, the brittle starkness of bare branches coated with frost. Jesus had these seasons, too—when he sweat blood in the Garden of Gethsemane, or when he suffered rejection and crucifixion on Calvary.

Other periods are full of blossoms and buds, vigor and hope: spiritual springs, like Jesus during the early part of his public life, being followed and admired by huge crowds as he preached and healed and performed miracles. Those springs are followed by seasons of waiting and guarding and weeding and watering: spiritual summers, like the latter period of our Lord's public life, when he spent time with his twelve apostles, keeping a lower profile because he was becoming so controversial. Harvest season comes, too—the Resurrection, the Ascension into heaven, the Holy Spirit-filled Pentecost.

Love Is Patient

Our mechanized, technology-driven world prepares us poorly for the seasons of spiritual growth. We are conditioned to expect immediate results, to be able to go to the spiritual grocery store and buy exactly what we need at any time, regardless of the season. We are conditioned by a consumer-centered, on-demand culture; we rebel at the spiritual realm, where humility and faith and wisdom can't be downloaded with the touch of a finger but must be asked for simply, sought after avidly, and cultivated perseveringly over various seasons of gestation.

It's hard to change our expectations, to travel life's pilgrimage at God's pace instead of trying to force him and ourselves to go at the world's 24/7-news-cycle pace. We all need to reflect frequently and deeply on this mysterious partnership between God's part and our part, between the seed and the soil. The Lord comes steadily and surely into our lives, transforming us gradually, the way that nature transforms a seed into a plant. We simply have to keep giving him the chance to do so.

St. James, who died a martyr's death at the hands of his own people in first-century Jerusalem, learned this lesson well. He wrote to the Christians of his time:

> *Be patient, therefore, brothers, until the coming of the Lord. See how the farmer waits for the precious fruit of the earth, being patient with it until it receives the early and the late rains. You too must be patient. Make your hearts firm, because the coming of the Lord is at hand.* (James 5:7–8)

Heeding the Call

Yet the most comforting lesson flowing from our Lord's parables about seeds and soil is the assurance that we are never alone in this work of following Christ and building his kingdom. The seed and the soil go together, always. God is not only our goal; he is also our companion, our light, our support, and our guide: "I am the way and the truth and the life.... I will not leave you orphans" (John 14:6; 14:18).

Certainly, God loves us too much to force our hand, but he also loves us too much to ever give up on us. He will always do his part, his 99 percent. But he will always respect our freedom, giving us space to do our part, our 1 percent. He will give us rest and comfort; he will make our lives fruitful; he will lead us into complete joy—but only if we heed his call, a heartfelt call that he never stops issuing: "Come to me…follow me…abide in me" (Matthew 11:28; 4:19; John 15:4, RSV). This is the great adventure, the joyful striving, the glorious toil of being a follower of Christ.

S

Questions for Personal Reflection or Group Discussion

1. What idea in this chapter struck you most and why?

2. Sometime today, read prayerfully the parable of the sower (Matthew 13:1–23), asking the Holy Spirit to show you what you need to see.

3. Reflect on your spiritual progress since you began to open your heart to God. What positive changes have you seen in yourself? Where would you most like to experience more growth? How would you describe the season you are currently in?

4. What will you do today to keep the soil of your heart ready to receive the seed of God's Word, in whatever form it comes?

    - I will take time away from the hustle and bustle just to be with God and let his love sink into my heart—maybe going for a quiet walk in a beautiful setting, or sitting silently in a chapel.
    - I will take a chunk of my drive time and simply sit in silence, reflecting on my life and asking God to speak to my heart, without listening to anything or talking on the phone.
    - I will finally do that kind but inconvenient deed that has been nagging my conscience for a while now, but that I have been trying to ignore.
    - (Write your own resolution) I will______________________________.

Concluding Prayer

Let nothing trouble you,
Let nothing frighten you,
Everything passes; God never changes.
Patience obtains all;
Whoever has God wants for nothing;
God alone is enough.
—A prayer by St. Teresa of Avila[4]

4 Prayer of St. Teresa of Avila, quoted in CCC, 227

Chapter 5
Full Freedom

The commitment to imitating Christ is the triumph of God's love that takes hold of a man and demands of him every possible effort in the service of this love, while at the same time he stays fully aware of human weakness.
—St. John Paul II, Homily, October 29, 1995

DIFFERENT PERSONALITIES TEND to react to this truth about our partnership with God in different ways. If carried to the extreme, these reactions can lead to a lack of interior balance, inhibiting the "glorious freedom of the children of God" (Romans 8:21) that we are called to begin experiencing even as we travel along our pilgrimage in this fallen world. Each of us needs to develop an awareness of how these tendencies show up in our own case, so as to gradually develop a healthy sense of balance while our interior freedom matures.

The Achiever's Trap

High achievers and perfectionists will tend to overemphasize the 1 percent that is our part. They can interpret the parable of the sower and the seed, and other parables of the kingdom, as threats. They tend to think that if they are not doing their absolute best at every moment, God won't be pleased and won't be able to send his grace. They feel that God is watching closely over them, but more analytically than lovingly. They can fall into subconsciously perceiving God as if he were a judge in a gymnastics competition, paying special attention and taking a perverse delight in all the flaws, all the shortcomings, of their Christian performance. They forget what God himself has told us about his unconditional love, a love that doesn't have to be earned: "I have loved you with an everlasting love; I have continued my faithfulness to you" (Jeremiah 31:3, RSV).

If this tendency is given free rein, the spiritual life can gradually become twisted and oppressive. The sweet and jubilant fascination that accompanied the soul's first personal encounters with the Lord gets worn down by fear, tension, and pressure, which are for the most part self-imposed. The deep, rich satisfaction that came from discovering the ultimate meaning of life (living in communion with God) and redirecting one's actions and desires toward that meaning, fades and almost disappears. The Christian quest for holiness comes to be felt as a stifling shackle and an exhaustive, unfair burden.

Unpleasant Repercussions

This path of overemphasizing our own efforts can have various eventual outcomes; the self-imposed pressure cooker can explode in a variety of directions. It can leave the soul brittle, harsh, and dry. This creates Christians who are pious but not holy, who are cold and judgmental and holier-than-thou. On the other hand, it can lead a person to rebel against God, to come to the conclusion that Christianity is nothing more than a spiritual and emotional prison constructed out of controlling lists of sadistic, inhuman obligations. The constant disappointment of not living up to unrealistic, self-imposed standards of performance can also lead to seemingly perennial discouragement, and even depression, paralyzing the soul or sparking addictions.

The Antidote

The tendency to overemphasize our own efforts needs to be balanced out by frequent contemplation of God's goodness, of his undying commitment to always be there with his 99 percent, and of his delight in our slightest efforts to put forth our 1 percent.

The achiever or perfectionist needs to think frequently and intentionally about all God has done through the ages, and all he continues to do, to further his loving plan of salvation. These individuals need to think frequently and intentionally of all God has done and continues to do to further their own individual stories of salvation. Like St. Paul, they need to renew their confidence in God, the senior partner of our Christian quest:

> *I am confident of this, that the one who began a good work in you will continue to complete it until the day of Christ Jesus.... For God is the one who, for his good purpose, works in you both to desire and to work. (Philippians 1:6; 2:13)*

The Lull of Mediocrity

For more social and spontaneous types, the tendency tilts to the other extreme: underemphasizing our role in spiritual growth. Casual and easy-going folks can fall into being lazy Christians, satisfied with comfortable mediocrity, because "God will take care of it."

Comfortable Christians habitually let their good, God-inspired resolutions languish and die. They may avoid the big dramatic sins, but they also avoid the taxing demands of mature love. They hear the Lord's call, and they feel the attraction of spiritual maturity (and sincerely desire it), but, like the rich young man in the Gospel who "went away sad" (Mark 10:22) after rejecting the Lord's invitation to leave behind his comfort zone, they have difficulty mustering up enough spiritual energy to keep on giving of themselves to God and neighbor until it hurts. They may not even allow themselves to consciously realize that they are resisting the nudge of grace.

Signs of Stagnation

Sometimes this tendency is hard to diagnose, because comfortable Christians are often jovial and quite engaged in good, holy activities that they enjoy. But they are not growing in their spiritual lives, because they are continually refusing, directly or indirectly, God's invitations to go deeper. They usually have good excuses, but their repeated refusals gradually create a kind of gray spiritual undertone in their lives, a hazy sense of inadequacy and dissatisfaction, a vague sadness lurking in the corners of their consciousness. This can even deepen into hidden but spiritually destructive self-loathing if the tendency fails to be identified and faced.

This underemphasizing of our part is hard to live with. So, comfortable

Christians frequently develop attachments to superficial pastimes that serve as distractions and temporary escape routes. God is continually calling out to them, because he never gives up on any of us. But they are afraid of answering the call and stepping out of their comfort zone, so they find ways to drown out that still, small voice.

Cultivating Courage

Comfortable Christians need to develop courage and perseverance. They need to allow the Holy Spirit to remind them of what's at stake in the spiritual battle. St. Paul is a sure guide in these reflections:

> *Working together, then, we appeal to you not to receive the grace of God in vain.... Work out your salvation with fear and trembling.... Let us not grow tired of doing good, for in due time we shall reap our harvest, if we do not give up. (2 Corinthians 6:1; Philippians 2:12; Galatians 6:9)*

Here again, contemplating God's goodness can provide powerful fuel for growth: The more convinced we are of God's wisdom and love toward us, the better chance we will have of trusting him when he invites us to step into uncomfortable territory. And even if we just keep taking very little steps, he will work wonders: "Draw near to God, and he will draw near to you" (James 4:8).

S

Questions for Personal Reflection or Group Discussion

1. What idea in this chapter struck you most and why?

2. Which of the two tendencies discussed in this chapter is stronger in you? How can you tell?

3. How deeply do you consider and reflect on God's goodness and love toward you? In other words, who is God for you, and how deeply have you experienced his personal, unconditional love? Are there perhaps some interior blocks that make it hard for you to accept and feel God's personal love for you?

4. Whether you tend to fall into the Achiever's Trap or the Lull of Mediocrity, growing in intimacy with God requires counteracting those tendencies by forming habits of thought and behavior that correspond more harmoniously with the full truth of who you are in Christ. Forming new habits takes time (most experts say about forty days) and consistent, intentional effort. What new habit will you begin to form today to help you grow in the full freedom of the children of God?

    - Today, and every day for the next month, I will consciously choose to step out of my comfort zone at least one time, when my conscience nudges me to—whether by doing an inconvenient (to me) favor for someone, speaking the truth when it's risky, or reaching out to someone who ought to be reaching out to me.
    - Today I will begin a Journal of Glory, where every day I will write down at least one good thing that God did for me during the day in order to cultivate a deeper awareness of his goodness—whether allowing me to marvel at a beautiful sunset, to experience a small success, or simply to enjoy a pleasing coincidence.
    - (Write your own resolution) I will____________________________.

Concluding Prayer

Take, Lord, and receive all my liberty,
my memory, my understanding
and my entire will,
All I have and call my own.
You have given all to me.
To you, Lord, I return it.
Everything is yours; do with it what you will.
Give me only your love and your grace.
That is enough for me.

—A prayer from St. Ignatius of Loyola[5]

5 http://www.loyolapress.com/suscipe-prayer-saint-ignatius-of-loyola.htm.

PART II

Loving God with All My Heart

One of the scribes, when he came forward and heard them disputing and saw how well he had answered them, asked him, "Which is the first of all the commandments?"

Jesus replied, "The first is this: 'Hear, O Israel! The Lord our God is Lord alone! You shall love the Lord your God with all your heart, with all your soul, with all your mind, and with all your strength.' The second is this: 'You shall love your neighbor as yourself.' There is no other commandment greater than these." (Mark 12:28–31)

Chapter 6
Loving with My All

I praise the Lord with you, because he is so great and beautiful a Love as to deserve the priceless gift of the whole person in the unfathomable depths of the heart, and in the concrete unfolding of daily duty through the various stages of life.
—St. John Paul II, Homily, February 2, 2002

THE MERE FACT that you are reading this book—and have gotten this far—should fill you with deep, intense joy. It shows that you already desire the most important thing: to know, love, and follow Jesus Christ more fully every day. That desire is supernatural. You couldn't have stirred it up on your own. Its presence in your soul shows without any doubt that God is with you and acting in your life. The engine of holiness is already humming in the depths of your heart, just as it was for the Blessed Virgin Mary. As the Preface of the Mass for Advent puts it: "...The Virgin Mother longed for him with love beyond all telling." Your longing to love God more fully, even if it seems to be a small or dim longing way down in the basement of your being, is in itself a movement of a very deep love for him, a love that gives him immense pleasure.

The deep longing for fulfillment, the yearning to come closer to Christ, is itself the work of Christ. He plants good, holy desires in the human heart so that he can later fulfill them. Through this longing, God is drawing you closer to his divine heart, where you will find more than you could ever have imagined, where your most intense desires will be satisfied to overflowing. As St. Thomas Aquinas put it when commenting on the fullness of love that the faithful experience in heaven: "Eternal life is the perfect fulfilment of desire; in as much as each of the blessed will have more than he desired or hoped for."[6]

Knowing that God is leading us to this glorious, indescribable destination should be an ongoing source of encouragement for all of us, as it was for St. Paul: "What eye has not seen, and ear has not heard, and what has not entered the human heart, what God has prepared for those who love him…" (1 Corinthians 2:9). We have that to look forward to.

A Precise Totality of Love

Jesus summarized our part in the fulfillment of this longing when he gave us the two great commandments. But fulfilling those commandments requires understanding them. What exactly was Jesus trying to tell us when he commanded us: "You shall love the Lord, your God, with all your heart, with all your soul, with all your mind, and with all your strength"? This, according to our Lord, is the first and greatest commandment, which overflows into the second most important commandment, "You shall love your neighbor as yourself" (Mark 12:30–31, RSV).

We have two possible interpretations for the verse about loving God. First, Jesus may have simply been using many terms to say one thing: Love God totally! His use of the terms "heart, soul, mind, and strength" may have been simply a rhetorical device, a poetic way of expressing totality, emphasized by his fourfold repetition of the world "all."

Yet, on the other hand, Jesus may have been consciously referring to the different powers of the soul when he listed those four modes of loving God. He may have meant exactly what he said, giving us clear instructions about what mature love for God looks like: it fills and overflows from the four main dimensions of human nature—the heart, the emotions, the intelligence, and the will.

These two interpretations are not mutually exclusive. They actually complement each other. To love God totally means to love him with every fiber of one's being. And that means integrating every sector of one's life

6 St. Thomas Aquinas, *Exposition of the Apostle's Creed*, XII.

and every capacity of our human nature into a true friendship with Jesus Christ.

Beyond Self-Help Lists

The self-help industry tends to divide up the art of living. It promotes "five ways to become happy," and "seven tricks to get ahead," and "ten secrets to success." This is not necessarily a bad thing. Lists like these often contain excellent advice. And in the face of real life's real complexity, they provide a certain degree of clarity, order, and understanding. The Ten Commandments themselves follow a similar structure.

Yet, in the Christian tradition, the Ten Commandments have always been seen as guidelines that point out the bare minimum requirements for staying on the path to happiness. The essence of happiness goes beyond the bare minimum; it goes deeper. Full spiritual maturity can never consist in mechanically fulfilling a list of dos and don'ts. Jesus knows this. And so, without completely erasing the lists, he brings us to the deeper level, to a more unified vision.

Authentic love is the essence of happiness: loving God totally, with all the powers of our human nature, and expressing that love through concrete decisions in daily life, through treating others (God's children, created in God's image and likeness) with the same concern and proactivity that marks every person's spontaneous attitude toward oneself.

Four Arenas of Love

Jesus chooses to describe this total love for God by referring to four separate arenas, so to speak, in which that love can be developed and grown and shown. This was no mistake. Three of the four terms Jesus uses were also used in the Old Testament; they formed part of God's original revelation to Israel (see Deuteronomy 6:5). Jesus reiterates them. And so, surely they mean something. To penetrate this meaning will open up new possibilities in any Christian's life, because it will show concrete ways to channel every Christian's deep desire to love God more fully.

The following chapters will examine in depth each of these four arenas of love, showing how each of the four activates different powers built into human nature. Only by growing harmoniously in all four areas can we truly allow God's grace to transform every corner of our lives, gradually discovering the abundant life that Jesus identified as the goal of his life's mission: "I came so that they might have life, and have it more abundantly" (John 10:10).

Although we will examine each sector separately, it's important to keep in mind that they are all connected. What happens in the emotions, for example, reverberates in the mind and the heart, and the direction of our heart affects our will and our emotions, and so on. The human person is a unified whole, even though our human nature does indeed have various powers and faculties.

Savoring the Promise

But before branching into the distinctions between heart, soul, mind, and strength, we should pause and take some time to savor the promise hidden inside this first commandment—the promise that God's grace is working hard to bring us not merely to an earthly happiness that comes from following five secret tips, but rather to the full, glorious, and everlasting satisfaction of spiritual maturity. Here's how Pope Benedict XVI portrayed that maturity in the context of describing the implications of our faith in Jesus. Notice how his expression seems to brim over with joy, energy, and optimism, which is how all of us should approach the great adventure of growing in God's love:

> *Faith in the Lord is not something that affects only our minds, the realm of intellectual knowledge; rather, it is a change involving the whole of our existence: our feelings, heart, mind, will, body, emotions and human relationships. With faith, everything changes in us and for us, and it reveals clearly our future destiny, the truth of our vocation in history, the meaning of our lives, the joy of being pilgrims en route to our heavenly homeland.*[7]

7 Pope Benedict XVI, Wednesday Audience, October 17, 2012.

S

Questions for Personal Reflection or Group Discussion

1. What idea in this chapter struck you most and why?

2. When did you first start experiencing a desire to know, love, and follow Jesus Christ more fully? Remember and savor that moment of grace.

3. What things in your life tend to encourage that holy desire, and what tends to drain it?

4. Think about the activities and commitments coming up in the next twenty-four hours. Which ones will be most threatening to the interior equilibrium that flows from loving God with your all? Think now about how you can react to those things more wisely.

    - With someone I tend to get into arguments with, I will listen and ask questions to understand what he or she means before responding.
    - With work I don't enjoy but have to do, I will make the Sign of the Cross and begin with a prayer to Jesus to ask for strength.
    - With a strong temptation that I often end up giving in to, I will avoid putting myself in the situation where the temptation usually arises.
    - (Write your own resolution) I will ______________________________.

Concluding Prayer

Soul of Christ, be my sanctification.
Body of Christ, be my salvation.
Blood of Christ, fill all my veins.
Water from Christ's side, wash out my stains.
Passion of Christ, my comfort be.
O Good Jesus, listen to me!
In thy wounds I fain would hide,
Ne'er to be parted from thy side.
Guard me should the foe assail me.

Guide me when my life shall fail me.
Bid me come to thee above,
With the saints to sing thy love,
World without end. Amen.

—Anima Christi, a medieval Latin prayer,
translated by Blessed John Henry Cardinal Newman[8]

8 http://www.newmanreader.org/works/meditations/meditations8.html#return1.

Chapter 7
Focusing on the Heart

Today, on this Lord's Day, I wish to invite all those who are listening to my words, not to forget our immortal destiny: life after death—the eternal happiness of heaven, or the awful possibility of eternal punishment, eternal separation from God, in what the Christian tradition has called hell. There can be no truly Christian living without an openness to this transcendent dimension of our lives. "Both in life and death we are the Lord's" (Romans 14:8).

—St. John Paul II, Homily, September 13, 1987

THE FIRST ARENA of love that Jesus points out is the "heart." In all three New Testament versions of this greatest commandment, *heart* is always first on the list.

Sacred Scripture uses this term more than a thousand times, but never to refer simply to the biological organ. The term always has a fuller, more complete, and more spiritual cachet. With so many appearances, the word can't help but take on a variety of connotations, yet the core meaning always remains the same. The *heart* refers to the deepest center of the person, the irreplaceable and irreducible "I" of the unique human individual. All the other powers of human nature flow from and depend on the heart. A person can say, "my feelings, my decisions, my hopes, my desires, my thoughts..." But while all of those possessions belong to someone, the *heart* is the biblical term that refers to the core identity of that someone; it encompasses the substantive center of the possessor of everything else.

The *Catechism* explores the rich and evocative meaning of this term in its discussion of Christian prayer, and the mysterious origin of prayer:

> *According to Scripture, it is the* heart *that prays.... The heart is the dwelling-place where I am, where I live; according to the Semitic or biblical expression, the heart is the place "to which I withdraw." The heart is our hidden center, beyond the grasp of our reason and of others; only the Spirit of God can fathom the human heart and know it fully. The heart is the place of decision, deeper than our psychic drives. It is the place of truth, where we choose life or death. It is the place of encounter, because as image of God we live in relation: it is the place of covenant. (CCC,* 2562–63)

This is the heart. Jesus commands his followers to love him, in the first place, with all their heart. What does this mean?

The Treasure Hunt

Jesus gives us a revealing clue in another one of his discourses, when he says, "For where your treasure is, there also will your heart be" (Matthew 6:21).

A treasure is what we value most, what we desire most, what we set our sights on attaining or maintaining. To love God with all our heart, therefore, means to make God—communion with him, friendship with him—into the overarching goal of our lives, into our most precious possession, into our deepest yearning. It means making our relationship with God the true north of our earthly journey, so that every decision, every desire, every hope and dream, every interpersonal interaction is evaluated, lived, and developed in light of that fundamental, orienting relationship.

As a result, anything that may damage our relationship with God must be cut away or re-dimensioned, especially sin and sinful habits, whereas anything that harmonizes with or may enhance our relationship with God is welcomed and integrated more and more fully into our life. As you can see, engaging the whole heart in our love for God is not something that happens from one moment to the next; it is a process. To love God with all your heart means intentionally and gradually making your relationship with him into the greatest—indeed, the only—treasure of your life.

Keep On Seeking

Loving God with all our heart means wanting, above everything else, to grow continually in our communion with him, in our friendship with him. This desire may start small, but as we grow, it also grows. And as our heart comes to love God more and more fully, every other desire is slowly but surely subordinated to and harmonized with that overarching desire, and so every experience, circumstance, and activity serves to bring us into a deeper knowledge of him. This is why Jesus was able to assure us, "Blessed are the clean of heart, for they will see God" (Matthew 5:8).

In the end, we get what we want. If we truly want God, if our heart is set on pursuing God, on seeking him, on living in a deeper and deeper communion with him, God will not deny us that treasure, which is called heaven—after all, that's what he created us for. This is why he can solemnly promise: "Seek and you will find" (Matthew 7:7). In the original Greek, the verb *seek* has the sense of an ongoing process: "Keep on seeking, and you will find." If we keep our hearts pointed toward God, we will reach full communion with God, wherein we find our happiness.

On the other hand, if we persistently prefer to seek our fulfillment in something else, in some idol—whether other relationships, achievements, or pleasures—leaving communion with God as a secondary concern, or as no concern at all, God will honor our choice. He will keep trying to convince us to set aside our idols in favor of his friendship, but he won't force us to do so. If we keep declining his invitations to the end, the purpose for which we were created—living in communion with God—will be everlastingly frustrated, and this is called hell.

Two Kinds of People

C.S. Lewis put it simply and eloquently in his masterpiece, *The Great Divorce*, referring to our Lord's amazing promise about seeking and finding: "Ask and it will be given to you; seek and you will find; knock and the door will be opened to you. For everyone who asks, receives; and the one who seeks, finds; and to the one who knocks, the door will be opened" (Matthew 7:7–8). Lewis comments on that dictum as follows:

> *There are only two kinds of people in the end: those who say to God, "Thy will be done," and those to whom God says, in the end, "Thy will be done." All that are in Hell, choose it. Without that self-choice there could be no Hell. No soul that seriously and constantly desires joy will ever miss it. Those who seek find. To those who knock it is opened.*[9]

When Jesus commands us to love God with all our heart, he is teaching us the right answer to the very first question he asked in the Gospel of John, a question that each of us must answer anew every single day of our lives: "What are you looking for?" (John 1:38). Where am I hoping to find the happiness I cannot resist desiring? If I hope to find it in God, I am loving God with my heart. As I progressively learn to hope to find it in *God alone*, and to order all the other smaller loves of my heart around that greatest love, I am learning to love God with *all* my heart.

S

Questions for Personal Reflection or Group Discussion

1. What idea in this chapter struck you most and why?

2. When you look into the depths of your soul, how do you answer Christ's question: "What are you looking for?"

3. If an independent observer were to follow you around for a typical week of your life, what would they conclude you are looking for in life?

4. Here on earth we find ourselves filled with conflicting desires. Even though, on the one hand, we do sincerely desire God, we also experience less worthy desires that often pop up uninvited. This is not reason for discouragement. God understands what you're made of! He will help you increase your good, God-centered desires, and purify the others. You just have to work with him. Today, what will you do to nourish your hope in God as the source of your lasting happiness?

   - I will take ten minutes to write down the most beautiful and satisfying

9 C.S. Lewis, *The Great Divorce: Collected Letters of C.S. Lewis*; (New York: HarperCollins, Kindle edition 2009) location 731–734.

experiences I have ever had—and then reflect on how they are connected to God as Creator, Redeemer, and Father and his love for me.

- After each meal today, I will say a short but sincere prayer of thanks before getting up from the table.
- (Write your own resolution) I will_____________________________.

Concluding Prayer

Be Thou my Vision, O Lord of my heart;
Naught be all else to me, save that Thou art
Thou my best Thought, by day or by night,
Waking or sleeping, Thy presence my light.

Be Thou my Wisdom, and Thou my true Word;
I ever with Thee and Thou with me, Lord;
Thou my great Father, I Thy true son;
Thou in me dwelling, and I with Thee one.

Be Thou my battle Shield, Sword for the fight;
Be Thou my Dignity, Thou my Delight;
Thou my soul's Shelter, Thou my high Tower:
Raise Thou me heavenward, O Power of my power.

Riches I heed not, nor man's empty praise,
Thou mine Inheritance, now and always:
Thou and Thou only, first in my heart,
High King of Heaven, my Treasure Thou art.

High King of Heaven, my victory won,
May I reach Heaven's joys, O bright Heaven's Sun!
Heart of my own heart, whatever befall,
Still be my Vision, O Ruler of all.

—Irish monastic prayer from the sixth century

Chapter 8
My Deepest Desire

St. Paul reminds us of two fundamental truths: first, that our ultimate vocation is to glorify the God who created and redeemed us; and secondly, that our eternal and highest good is to "attain to the fullness of God himself" (Ephesians 3:19)—to participate in the loving communion of the Father and the Son and the Holy Spirit for all eternity. God's glory and our good are perfectly attained in the kingdom of heaven.

—St. John Paul II, Homily, September 18, 1987

LOVING GOD WITH all one's heart simply means making God—an increasing communion with him, an ever-deepening friendship with him—the highest priority and guiding principle of one's life. It is love understood as the fundamental desire, the fundamental orientation of one's life.

When Jesus began his public ministry with a call to conversion, this is what he was getting at. By announcing that "the kingdom of God is at hand" (Mark 1:15), he was pointing out that in him, God-become-man, full communion with God is now truly possible. God has made himself one of us, so that we can enter into a real friendship with him. Jesus is Emmanuel, God with us. Before Jesus, God was close to his people, but it was a closeness always mediated by something: by creation, by his revelation and his commandments, by his prophets.

In Jesus, who is truly God and truly man, God's closeness has taken a definitive turn, and we can love God with all our heart truly, through a fully human relationship with the eternal God, through knowing and following the Son. All it takes is leaving behind any idols, any fundamental desire that can't be subordinated to or harmonized with the desire to live in communion with God: "Repent, and believe in the gospel!" (Mark 1:15).

Running to Win

A healthy professional football team has one overarching goal, one fundamental desire: to win the championship. All the decisions made by the coaches and players are made with that in mind. All the activities they engage in, all the sacrifices they make, all the intermediate objectives and challenges, are seen and dealt with in light of that goal. That goal is the ultimate source of the entire team's dynamism, effort, and yearnings. The championship is the treasure they are hunting and hoping for; everything else takes on meaning through its relationship with that treasure.

St. Paul draws a parallel between this kind of all-encompassing, athletic treasure hunt and a Christian's hunt for greater and greater intimacy with Christ here on earth and the definitive, total communion with him forever in heaven:

> *Do you not know that the runners in the stadium all run in the race, but only one wins the prize? Run so as to win. Every athlete exercises discipline in every way. They do it to win a perishable crown, but we an imperishable one. Thus I do not run aimlessly; I do not fight as if I were shadowboxing. No, I drive my body and train it, for fear that, after having preached to others, I myself should be disqualified. (1 Corinthians 9:24–27)*

When I love God with all my heart, my relationship with him becomes the axis of my activity, the magnet that brings order and dynamism into all the otherwise scattered shards of my life, the organizing principle around which every other element is arranged.

Love's Purifying Fire

This is how love for God purifies us. As we allow ourselves to be drawn more fully into friendship with him, we let go of unhealthy attachments that are holding us back from spiritual maturity. We leave behind selfish habits, behaviors, and attitudes that feel comfortable, or maybe even necessary, but that in fact impede us from loving and living with full freedom. We leave them behind, because our growing intimacy with God leaves no room for them.

This is the "discipline" that St. Paul calls Christians to exercise. The Letter to the Hebrews echoes St Paul's comparison of spiritual growth to running a race, while emphasizing more this purifying effect of a growing, heartfelt love for God:

> *Let us rid ourselves of every burden and sin that clings to us and persevere in running the race that lies before us while keeping our eyes fixed on Jesus, the leader and perfecter of faith.* (Hebrews *12:1–2)*

Sometimes this purification requires renouncing material objects, but it can never be only that. Material poverty in itself is no virtue. Poverty of spirit, the purity of our fundamental desire, is what matters. As St. Thomas Aquinas explained it, "It is abundantly clear that the human heart is more intensely attracted to one object, in proportion as it is withdrawn from a multiplicity of desires."[10] In other words, I can better focus my attention on one task if I am not distracted by trying to do five other tasks at the same time.

Tanto Cuanto

St. Ignatius of Loyola explored this aspect of loving God with all our heart in his famous meditation about *tanto cuanto*. That Spanish phrase can be translated "inasmuch as." St. Ignatius points out that everything in creation, from mountains to moods, from galaxies to good food, from rehearsals to relationships, is given to us by God out of love and for love. All these things are essentially good, and they exist to be a stepping stone toward greater intimacy with God, to be opportunities for experiencing God's love for us and for showing and growing our love for him. In as much as we enjoy and use all things for that purpose, they are good for us. But if we turn any of God's gifts into idols, seeking our fulfillment in them instead of in loving God through them, they become bad.

---

10 St. Thomas Aquinas, *De Perfectione Vitae Spiritualis*, VI.

To take a rather mundane example, watching football on the weekends is not intrinsically evil. It can be a healthy form of recreation. But when it impedes me from fulfilling my basic responsibilities—like attending to family needs or worshipping God on the Lord's Day—it has overstepped its bounds and become an obstacle, a little idol.

Jesus himself illustrated this principle with his parables of the treasure in the field and the pearl of great price. The treasure and the pearl symbolize the kingdom of God, our friendship with Christ, our living in communion with him. All other realities are given to us to help us achieve and deepen that communion.

> *The kingdom of heaven is like a treasure buried in a field, which a person finds and hides again, and out of joy goes and sells all that he has and buys that field. Again, the kingdom of heaven is like a merchant searching for fine pearls. When he finds a pearl of great price, he goes and sells all that he has and buys it. (Matthew 13:44–46)*

Loving God with all our heart means living in accordance with the truth of our treasure. Nothing matters more than our relationship with God. We believe that, and so we desire nothing more than an ever-deepening intimacy with him. And we spend our lives learning to live accordingly.

S

Questions for Personal Reflection or Group Discussion

1. What idea in this chapter struck you most and why?

2. What evidence is there in your daily life to show that you are "running to win"? What evidence is there in your daily life to show that you are not really "running to win"?

3. Are there any attachments in your life (possessions, dreams, relationships, habits) that are holding you back from loving God with all your heart?

4. Many of us have a tendency to clutter our lives with lots of things that we don't really need, things that weigh us down in our pursuit of

spiritual maturity instead of propelling us forward. What will you "rid yourself of" today that will free your heart to love God a little bit more fully?

- I will spend less time surfing the Web, chatting through social media, or indulging in entertainment.
- I will go through my closet and take out every outfit I haven't worn at least once in the last year and donate those clothes to someone who can use them.
- I will look over my credit-card bills from the last two months and see what kinds of whimsical purchases I can cut down on.
- (Write your own resolution) I will____________________________.

Concluding Prayer

Hear my voice, LORD, when I call;
have mercy on me and answer me.
"Come," says my heart, "seek his face";
your face, LORD, do I seek!
Do not hide your face from me;
do not repel your servant in anger.
You are my salvation; do not cast me off;
do not forsake me, God my savior!
Even if my father and mother forsake me,
the LORD will take me in...

—Psalm 27:7–10

Chapter 9
Nourishing My Heart

There is no doubt that spiritual formation ought to occupy a privileged place in a person's life. Everyone is called to grow continually in intimate union with Jesus Christ, in conformity to the Father's will, in devotion to others in charity and justice.

—St. John Paul II, *Christifideles Laici,* 60

LOVING GOD WITH all your heart means desiring him above all things and making your intimate, personal relationship with him into the highest priority of your life, the center around which every other facet of your existence finds its proper and glorious place. But how do you do that? How do you make that happen?

The heart expresses itself through the other three modes that Jesus identifies in the greatest commandment: loving God with all our soul, mind, and strength. Attending to each of those arenas, therefore, produces an indirect effect on the heart as well, educating and purifying it, and nourishing its Christian core. Nevertheless, you can also attend to the heart directly.

Thoughts of the Heart

We spend a lot of time thinking about the things we desire. When we treasure something, it occupies our mind. And, conversely, the more we think about something, the more we tend to desire it.

This is part of human nature; it flows from the connection between the two spiritual faculties that human nature possesses—intelligence and will, the power to know and the power to choose. For us human beings, these faculties utilize instruments to operate: our senses, our imagination, our memory, our emotions, and our passions. Unlike angels, whose access to truth and goodness is purely spiritual and immediate, human persons discover truth and goodness gradually, through the mediation of spatial-temporal experience. This is why we can figure out a solution to a complex problem by making diagrams and pictures, doodling, trying various alternatives in our imagination, and discussing it with others.

And so, what we choose to look at, think about, and daydream about will affect the desires that grow and mature in our heart. The intensity of our love for a certain object can increase or decrease according to how much attention we pay to that object and how much space it takes up in our external and internal senses (memory and imagination).

Tricks of the Devil

The devil understands this reality and uses it in the dynamics of temptation. St. James explains how temptation begins with something that stirs up a self-centered desire, and then, if we choose to pay attention to that desire, it grows. If we feed it with more attention, we will eventually act on it, committing sin. If we continue to act on it, the sin can become a habit and even choke off the life of grace:

> *Each person is tempted when he is lured and enticed by his own desire. Then desire conceives and brings forth sin, and when sin reaches maturity it gives birth to death. (James 1:14–15)*

The devil, agitating our fallen nature and the fallen world in which we live, will try to monopolize our attention with images, ideas, thoughts, and invitations that can lure us into self-absorption and eventually into destructive self-indulgence. The enemy of our souls wants to occupy our minds with a multiplicity of inputs that can divide our hearts, draining our desire for God and filling up our desires for any number of petty idols.

Spiritual Heart Supplements

Forming our heart in Christ follows the contrary path. To feed our desire for God and our desire to make our relationship with him the core and fountain of everything we do requires thinking frequently about him and his magnificent plan for our lives. Just as a little boy will feed his desire for a new bike by looking at a picture of that bike every day, so too we need to gaze at the Lord and savor his dream for us as often as we can. We need to feed the central desire of our Christian heart with thoughts that are in harmony with that desire. And we need to intentionally stir up those thoughts all the time. The Psalms frequently make choosing to think about God and his plans (his name, promise, judgments, testimonies) a central theme for prayer:

> *In my heart I treasure your promise, that I may not sin against you.... At all times my soul is stirred with longing for your judgments.... Direct my heart toward your testimonies and away from gain. Avert my eyes from what is worthless; by your way give me life. When I recite your judgments of old...I am comforted, LORD. Even at night I remember your name in observance of your law, LORD. (Psalm 119:11, 20, 36–37, 52, 55)*

Most of the traditional pious practices associated with Christianity have this as their goal. Displaying images of Jesus, Mary, and the saints on our walls, desks, rearview mirrors, and screen savers; wearing a cross or a crucifix around our necks; wearing blessed medals; dropping by a church and making the Sign of the Cross with holy water; asking for a priest's blessing; praying before meals.... Practices like these set reminders for us to think about God. They can nourish the core desire of our hearts.

Eating Right

But the meat and potatoes of forming the Christian heart remain prayer and the sacraments (we will dive into these realities more fully in later chapters). Without a real, growing life of prayer—in all of its forms, but most essentially in a daily, personal God-time—our core desire for God will always remain undernourished, and our spiritual growth will be stunted. Infrequent or superficial contact with the sacraments, especially the Eucharist and confession, robs our souls of essential spiritual nutrients. Jesus made this clear so many times:

> *On Prayer: "Then Jesus told them a parable about the necessity for them to pray always without becoming weary…"* (Luke 18:1); *"If you remain in me and my words remain in you, ask for whatever you want and it will be done for you."* (John 15:7)

> *On the Eucharist: "Jesus said to them, 'Amen, amen, I say to you, unless you eat the flesh of the Son of Man and drink his blood, you do not have life within you. Whoever eats my flesh and drinks my blood has eternal life, and I will raise him on the last day. For my flesh is true food, and my blood is true drink. Whoever eats my flesh and drinks my blood remains in me and I in him. Just as the living Father sent me and I have life because of the Father, so also the one who feeds on me will have life because of me.'"* (John 6:53–57)

> *On confession (Jesus to his apostles): "Whose sins you forgive are forgiven them, and whose sins you retain are retained."* (John 20:23)

God himself gives us a new heart when we become Christians, but he leaves it up to us to make that heart grow.

S

Questions for Personal Reflection or Group Discussion

1. What idea in this chapter struck you most and why?

2. Are you a better pray-er than you were a year ago, five years ago, ten years ago? Why or why not?

3. In a normal day, how often do you think about God and his plan for your life and for the world?

4. An old Native American story tells of a young brave talking with an elderly warrior. The old warrior explains that there are two wolves fighting a fierce battle against each other inside every human heart. One wolf fights to destroy all that is good through indulging in greed, lust, and cowardice. The other one fights to protect all that is good through fighting greed, lust, and cowardice. The young brave asks his elder which wolf will win the fight, and the wise warrior replies: "Whichever one you feed." What will you do today to feed the core desire of your life, the desire to make your relationship with God the organizing principle of everything you do?

    - I will replace superficial images on my walls, desk, screen saver, and mobile devices with images that really mean something.
    - I will take some time in the evening to reflect, prayerfully, on my behavior during the day, identifying how I can better reflect God's goodness tomorrow.
    - I will avoid reading or watching things that cause unhealthy turbulence or distraction in my soul.
    - (Write your own resolution) I will__________________________.

Concluding Prayer

O God, let me know you and love you so that I may find my joy in you; and if I cannot do so fully in this life, let me at least make some progress every day, until at last that knowledge, love and joy come to me in all their plenitude.

While I am here on earth let me learn to know you better, so that in heaven I may know you fully; let my love for you grow deeper here, so that there I may love you fully.

On earth then I shall have great joy in hope, and in heaven complete joy in the fulfillment of my hope.

—from the *Proslogion* of St. Anselm of Canterbury

Chapter 10
Freeing My Heart

Undoubtedly, the journey is arduous; it demands availability, courage, self-denial, in order to make one's life, as Christ did his, a "gift" of love to the Father and to others. Only in this way are we made capable, by the power of the Spirit, of proclaiming the "Gospel of the Cross" and carrying out that "new evangelization" that has in Christ crucified and risen its center and hinge.

—St. John Paul II, Homily, February 24, 1991

IN HIS PARABLE of the sower and the seed, Jesus pointed out that having good soil is not sufficient to assure fruitful growth. Some seed fell on excellent soil, but it shared that soil with thorn bushes. The thorn bushes grew with the good seed and choked it. Jesus draws the lesson from his analogy: "As for the seed that fell among thorns, they are the ones who have heard, but as they go along, they are choked by the anxieties and riches and pleasures of life, and they fail to produce mature fruit" (Luke 8:14).

The anxieties and riches and pleasures of life aren't evil in themselves. The problem comes when we allow them to divide our hearts, when we begin seeking them, instead of seeking God, or paying more attention to them than to God. Jesus is trying to warn us about what will happen to our spiritual life when we allow contradictory desires to coexist in our heart, when we feed multiple desires, instead of feeding the one core desire and allowing that desire to bring all subordinate desires into harmony. He wants us to stay focused: "But seek first the kingdom (of God) and his righteousness, and all these things will be given you besides" (Matthew 6:33).

We need to nourish the Christ-centered desire at the core of our Christian heart, but we also need to protect that desire from thorns and parasites and other distractions that can starve it out.

The One Thing Needed

One of the Lord's most memorable teaching moments arose in this context. He and his apostles had been invited to dine at the home of Martha of Bethany. Martha was busy keeping everyone happy. She was perturbed that her sister, Mary, wasn't helping her. You probably remember what happened:

> *As they continued their journey he entered a village where a woman whose name was Martha welcomed him. She had a sister named Mary [who sat] beside the Lord at his feet listening to him speak. Martha, burdened with much serving, came to him and said, "Lord, do you not care that my sister has left me by myself to do the serving? Tell her to help me." The Lord said to her in reply, "Martha, Martha, you are anxious and worried about many things. There is need of only one thing. Mary has chosen the better part and it will not be taken from her" (Luke 10:38–42).*

Notice that Jesus didn't reprimand Martha for being busy, or for doing a lot of things, but for being "anxious and worried about many things." Martha was upset. Where did that come from? Clearly, she was not desiring only and principally the "one thing" needed—communion with God. In the hustle and bustle of entertaining, she had allowed her heart to be divided. She had become overly preoccupied with making a good impression by having everything come out just right. A tinge of vanity had temporarily upended the true priorities of her heart, leading her to overemphasize secondary things. She resented Mary for not sharing her desire to make the evening go perfectly according to plan. She lashed out at her sister in a typical family squabble.

Whenever we allow self-centered desires to compete with, instead of being purified and ordered by, the one desire that we really need, we fall into the same trap.

Pulling Big Weeds

The lesson is clear. We not only need to nourish our desire for God, we also need to keep the soil of our heart free from suffocating, contradictory desires. This takes two forms of spiritual discipline.

First, we need to uproot the thorns that are already growing in our souls. These include obvious sinful habits, like losing our temper, procrastinating, gossiping, using pornography, lying, cheating, abusing alcohol or drugs, and all the other destructive behaviors that flow from the seven capital sins of gluttony, lust, anger, sloth, arrogance, envy, and greed.

These are behaviors that the fallen world tolerates, and even encourages. Popular culture glorifies them in music, film, and advertising. But they are poison for the heart. They destroy and enslave us and those we love. They are sins because they are evil, because they go directly against everything that will make us flourish as human beings created in God's image.

Battles between Flesh and Spirit

St. Paul refers to these sins as the desires of our "flesh." Flesh in this context doesn't mean our bodies, our materiality, which is fundamentally good because it is created by God. Rather, it means our fallen nature, our wounded human nature that pulls us away from the path of life in God's Spirit.

> *I say, then: live by the Spirit and you will certainly not gratify the desire of the flesh. For the flesh has desires against the Spirit, and the Spirit against the flesh.... Now the works of the flesh are obvious: immorality, impurity, licentiousness, idolatry, sorcery, hatreds, rivalry, jealousy, outbursts of fury, acts of selfishness, dissensions, factions, occasions of envy, drinking bouts, orgies, and the like. I warn you, as I warned you before, that those who do such things will not inherit the kingdom of God.* (Galatians 5:16–21)

Because tendencies toward these behaviors are rooted deep within us (often connected to emotional wounds that we are barely aware of) and continuously stimulated by influences all around us, uprooting the thorns of sinful habits can be a long and difficult process. Traditionally, this phase of spiritual growth is called the purgative, or purification, stage.

Pulling Little Weeds

As the soil of our hearts is cleared of the big thorn bushes, we can focus more on watering and fertilizing the good desire for God, which is the topic of the rest of this book. But even then, we have to keep a lookout for the return of new weeds—this is the second spiritual discipline that keeps our heart's soil clean and rich. It involves sub-disciplines such as making room for silence in our daily lives, including some voluntary austerity in our lifestyle, keeping a healthy balance between work and rest, being more and more intentional as regards the kind of input we allow into our minds and imaginations—choosing, for example, types of entertainment and recreation that both delight and also edify. If we are careless in these little things, the weeds will surely come back, and the thorns will choke the precious core desire of the Christ-centered heart.

S

Questions for Personal Reflection or Group Discussion

1. What idea in this chapter struck you most and why?

2. What big weeds has God uprooted from your life in the past? Thank him for that grace. Are there any big weeds still choking your relationship with God? Ask him for the light and strength to root them out.

3. What types of situations typically make you "worried and anxious"? Why? Speak with God about any desires or fears that may be dividing your heart.

4. One of the greatest dangers for our spiritual growth is falling into routine. When we lose sight of the real purpose of our lives, of God's dream for us, we can just get stuck in a rut, doing the same things

over again, and maybe even doing them well but without the zest of consciously remembering how they fit into God's bigger picture. What will you do differently today to activate your desire to "seek first the kingdom of God"?

- I will serve someone who usually serves me.
- I will re-read something from my past (a diary or journal entry, a letter, an old essay) that will stir up afresh the best dreams of my heart.
- (Write your own resolution) I will____________________________.

Concluding Prayer

Too late have I loved you, O Beauty so ancient, O Beauty so new.
Too late have I loved you!
You were within me but I was outside myself,
and there I sought you!
In my weakness I ran after
the beauty of the things you have made.
You were with me, and I was not with you.
The things you have made kept me from you—the things which
would have no being unless they existed in you!
You have called, you have cried,
and you have pierced my deafness.
You have radiated forth, you have shined out brightly,
and you have dispelled my blindness.
You have sent forth your fragrance, and I have breathed it in,
and I long for you.
I have tasted you, and I hunger and thirst for you.
You have touched me, and I ardently desire your peace.

—St. Augustine of Hippo[11]

11 *Confessions*, Book X

PART III
Loving God with All My Soul

My child, when you come to serve the Lord, prepare yourself for trials. Be sincere of heart and steadfast, and do not be impetuous in time of adversity. Cling to him, do not leave him, that you may prosper in your last days. Accept whatever happens to you; in periods of humiliation be patient. For in fire gold is tested, and the chosen, in the crucible of humiliation. Trust in God, and he will help you; make your ways straight and hope in him. (Sirach 2:1–6)

Chapter 11
Weak but Wonderful

But here is the great surprise: God has given the human person, the weak creature, a wonderful dignity: he has made him a little less than the angels or, as the original Hebrew can be translated, a little less than a god.
—St. John Paul II, General Audience, June 26, 2002

THORNS CAN CHOKE the growth of the good seed of God's grace, but shallow, rocky soil can wither it altogether. Jesus warned us of this, too. He used the analogy of bad soil that impedes a seed from putting down deep roots. Under the scorching sun, the plant simply withers and dies, because its shallow roots fail to find the moisture it needs for life under harsh conditions. The image describes the sentimental Christian, whose faith only goes as deep as his or her feelings:

> *The seed sown on rocky ground is the one who hears the word and receives it at once with joy. But he has no root and lasts only for a time. When some tribulation or persecution comes because of the word, he immediately falls away.* (Matthew 13:20–21)

Feelings, emotions, sentiments, and moods, along with psychic and biological drives, passions, and needs, make up an essential dimension of human experience. When Jesus commands his followers to love him with all their *soul*, he is referring to this wonderful, confusing, rewarding, and troubling dimension. If we fail to integrate this human richness into our loving relationship with God, sooner or later it will trip us up, and our desire for God and a deeper communion with him will wither away.

In the Old Testament, for example, King David failed to integrate healthily a natural and passionate attraction he felt toward a woman who was married to another man. This failure led him into the destructive moral chaos of adultery and murder. In the New Testament, we see how St. Peter's natural and understandable emotional fears, improperly acknowledged and channeled, led him to commit the most shameful deed of his life when he denied that he even knew Jesus (see Matthew 26:69–75).

The two-thousand-year tradition of Christian thought and experience has produced a deep, nuanced, and accurate understanding of these various facets of the human person. Becoming more aware of them frees us to be more intentional and effective in our journey toward spiritual maturity.

X-Ray of a Soul

Soul can be a confusing word. People often ask whether their dog has a soul. The answer often comes back as a simple no, which is disappointing, because people really want their loyal, beloved pets to be with them in heaven. But how can a dog get to heaven if it doesn't have a soul? We will set aside for now the theological question of whether pets join us in heaven; suffice it to say that if you need the accompaniment of a beloved pet in order to be absolutely, completely, infinitely happy (that's what life is like in heaven), you will not lack that pet.

Philosophically, though, we can give a better answer to the question of whether dogs have souls. Yes, they do have souls, but their souls are different than the human soul. Specifically, the soul is the principle of life in a living being. Anything alive, then, has a soul. But the different forms of life will have souls with different characteristics. Plants have nutritive souls that allow them to grow and reproduce, but without the power of locomotion. Animals have what are called sensitive souls. These add new powers to the nutritive souls, especially the powers of locomotion and sensory perception. These powers allow the more complex animal species (dolphins, for example, are more complex than spiders) to experience certain degrees of emotion, sense memory, and sense knowledge.

Human beings have rational souls, with the even greater additional powers of intellect and will, abstract thinking and free choice. These are spiritual powers shared in a certain way with the angels and with God himself. This is one reason why the Bible speaks of God having created the human person in the image of God: "in our image, after our likeness" (Genesis 1:26). These spiritual powers that go with personhood, integrally united to the other nutritive and sensitive powers still present in the human soul, are the root of human dignity. They show us why it is morally okay to kill a bothersome mosquito, but not a bothersome toddler.

Problems with the Soul

Those basic philosophical distinctions have been challenged in modern and post-modern times. Biologists have discovered so many varieties of life that were completely unknown to previous eras, for example, that the distinctions between vegetative and locomotive, or between sentient and nutritive, are much more fluid. Viruses, bacteria, extremophile—where do they all fit into the continuum between simple plant and complex animal? It's not always easy to tell.

Post-modern secularists also question the distinction between spiritual and non-spiritual souls. Many of them argue that what used to be considered spiritual is really just epiphenomenal, just an excretion of predetermined material and biological processes. According to this point of view, the human soul is no more spiritual, and therefore possesses no more dignity, than any other animal soul. The difference between a human being and a dolphin, therefore, is only a difference of degree, not a difference of kind.

These challenges to the Christian vision of the human person can be and have been met and overcome by Christian philosophers, scientists, and apologists. And their arguments simply reinforce the basic tenets of our faith, the basic truths revealed by God, that the human soul is unique among the many creatures of the visible universe, and uniquely valued and addressed by God.

The Beloved Soul

Before we love at all, we are loved, infinitely and intimately, utterly and unconditionally, passionately and personally, by God. This must be the starting place for our reflection on what it means to love God with all our soul. Every component of our humanity is included in this love God has for us. The greatest proof of this astounding truth came with the Incarnation, when God himself took on human nature, becoming fully and truly man in Jesus Christ. Never again can we doubt that every aspect of the human condition, even though tangled and distorted by sin, is fundamentally good, and that God wants to redeem it all.

We have to consciously give ourselves permission, so to speak, to accept this truth. Otherwise, the difficult and often painful process of allowing God's grace to bring order and healing to the dizzying complexity of our souls may spark discouragement or resentment.

The *Catechism* announces our fundamental dignity and belovedness loud and clear:

> *Of all visible creatures only man is "able to know and love his creator." He is "the only creature on earth that God has willed for its own sake," and he alone is called to share, by knowledge and love, in God's own life. It was for this end that he was created, and this is the fundamental reason for his dignity. (CCC, 356)*

In his inaugural homily, Pope Benedict XVI expressed the same truth with even more gusto:

> *We are not some casual and meaningless product of evolution. Each of us is the result of a thought of God. Each of us is willed, each of us is loved, each of us is necessary.*[12]

S

Questions for Personal Reflection or Group Discussion

1. What idea in this chapter struck you most and why?

2. When you consider the truth that God loves you personally and infinitely, how deeply does it resonate? Is there something in you that sometimes resists accepting that truth?

12 Benedict XVI, Homily, April 24, 2005.

3. How much do your emotional ups and downs affect the firmness of your faith? Do you only pray when you feel like it? Do you only forgive and show kindness when you are in a good mood? How often do bad moods and emotional low tides lead you to say and do things you later regret?

4. In spite of our weakness and brokenness, God loves us without limit. Jesus once told St. Faustina that even if she had on her soul all the sins of the world, in comparison with his mercy they would be nothing more than a drop of water thrown into a blazing furnace. What will you do today to express your faith in your true, God-given dignity and that of every human person?

    - I will take a break to stop and smell the roses (to enjoy one of the simple, healthy pleasures of life), and I will thank God for that blessing.
    - I will pray sincerely for a person that I have given up on.
    - I will engage in sincere conversation with someone that I normally wouldn't talk to.
    - (Write your own resolution) I will____________________________.

Concluding Prayer

O LORD, our Lord,
how awesome is your name through all the earth!
I will sing of your majesty above the heavens
with the mouths of babes and infants.
You have established a bulwark against your foes,
to silence enemy and avenger.
When I see your heavens, the work of your fingers,
the moon and stars that you set in place —
What is man that you are mindful of him,
and a son of man that you care for him?
Yet you have made him little less than a god,
crowned him with glory and honor.
You have given him rule over the works of your hands,
put all things at his feet:

All sheep and oxen,
even the beasts of the field,
The birds of the air, the fish of the sea,
and whatever swims the paths of the seas.
O LORD, our Lord,
how awesome is your name through all the earth!

—Psalm 8

Chapter 12
Understanding Emotions

You live with great hopes, with so many fine plans for the future. But do not forget that the true fullness of life is to be found only in Christ, who died and rose again for us. Christ alone is able to fill in the deep space of the human heart. He alone gives the strength and joy of living, in spite of any limit or external impediment.

—St. John Paul II, Message for World Youth Day, 1989

JESUS SPECIFIES TWO innate powers of the human soul when he issues the great commandment: He commands us to love God with all our mind and all our strength. These correspond to the specifically spiritual powers of the soul—the intellect and will, our capacity to know and to choose. When he commands us to love God with all our soul, then, it is safe to assume that he is referring to the other powers of the soul. He is commanding us to align those with the core desire, with the heart that seeks God above all things, or that at least wants to seek God above all, because it knows and believes that "God alone suffices," as St. Theresa of Avila once put it. His command to love God with all our soul is an invitation to integrate our emotions and passions, or psychic drives, into our friendship with him so that the friendship can reach new heights. How do we do that? What does that look like?

The Gift of Emotions

Emotions come from God. God created human nature, and emotions are part of human nature. When we come into contact with external realities, we often perceive that those realities can help or harm us. That perception produces a reaction in our soul, a feeling that moves us toward action. We were created to function that way. We have this internal dynamism that attracts us toward what seems good for us and repels us from what seems bad for us. This is our capacity for feelings or emotions (sometimes called passions). Their complexity and intensity contribute to making human experience as rich and wonderful as it is.

Categories of Emotion

Through the ages, philosophers have identified basic emotions. In modern times, psychologists have offered numerous other classifications. So far, no one has come up with a perfect synthesis of the wisdom of the philosophers and the science of the psychologists. In our effort to understand emotions, we will utilize insights from both sources.

An unavoidable obstacle in this effort has to do with language. The words that describe emotions—which are simple reactions to stimuli, simple feelings that have no moral weight in themselves—are often the same words that can also describe moral actions, vices, or virtues. Anger, for example, can refer to the simple emotional reaction of feeling anger, something which is natural and good in itself. But the word *anger* can also refer to a capital sin, the sin of anger, of choosing to act unjustly, violently, and self-centeredly in response to the feeling of anger. This language problem has no easy solution, so keep in mind that this discussion of feelings will use words such as *anger* (and *love*, and *hate*, and *desire*) strictly as emotional descriptors, not as moral terms linked to virtue and vice.

The Nine Most Basic Emotions

The nine basic emotions flow from the two contrary, foundational urges of our embodied human nature, which Christian philosophy labels *love* and *hate*. At their most fundamental level, these urges are connected to our senses and our bodies, and they are morally neutral; they are simple, emotional reactions to exterior stimuli; they are spontaneous feelings of love and hate without any moral decision to love or hate. Certain things in the world are good for us, and the urge of love, or attraction, kicks into gear when we come into contact with those things. Certain other things in the world are bad for us, and the urge of hate, or repulsion, kicks into gear when we come into contact with those things.

THE NINE BASIC EMOTIONS

Emotions Deriving from Fundamental Urge of Love or Attraction		Emotions Deriving from Fundamental Urge of Hate or Repulsion	
GOOD (HELPFUL) OBJECT IS...	RESULTING EMOTION:	BAD (HARMFUL) OBJECT IS...	RESULTING EMOTION:
Simply perceived	*Desire*	Simply perceived	*Desire*
Perceived as difficult but possible to attain	*Hope/anticipation*	Simply present	*Sorrow*
Perceived as impossible to attain	*Despair/dejection*	Perceived as present but possible to overcome	*Anger*
Attained/possessed	*Pleasure/joy*	Perceived as somewhat distant but hard to avoid	*Fear*
		Perceived as somewhat distant but avoidable	*Courage/audacity*

The experience of attraction stirs up four of the nine basic emotions. When we perceive something that would be good for us, we feel a desire for it. Desire—this is the first basic emotion. When that good, desirable thing seems as if it will be hard to acquire, but we think that if we make an effort, we will indeed acquire it, we feel the basic emotion of hope (the feeling, not the virtue). If the good, desirable thing seems impossible to acquire, we experience a feeling of despair, discouragement, or hopelessness (again, just the feeling, not the sin). When we actually acquire the good, desirable thing and are enjoying it, we feel pleasure, the fourth emotion connected to the urge of attraction.

The experience of repulsion stirs up the other five basic emotions. If we perceive something that will harm us, some evil thing, we feel the basic emotion of aversion, or revulsion. If that hateful thing actually comes upon us or happens to us, we feel sorrow or pain. If it comes upon us and we judge that by resisting we can actually get rid of it, we feel anger (the emotion, not the sin). If the hateful thing is out there somewhere and seems hard for us to avoid, we experience fear. If the hateful thing out there seems hard to avoid, but we judge that we can indeed avoid or eliminate it, we experience feelings of courage or audacity.

Emotion in Action

A few simple examples will help clarify. If I am hungry and I see a ripe apple in the fruit basket (and if I like apples), I will feel *desire*—the good, desirable apple is perceived as something that will help me. If the last time I took that kind of apple out of that particular basket, it had a big, fat worm in it, I may feel *revulsion* when I see that apple, which by association I perceive as something that may harm me. If I am penniless and hungry and see a basketful of apples at the store, I may feel *hope* if there is some way I can get enough money to buy one, and I may feel *despair* if I can't think of any way to get any money. If I get the money and I am on the way to the store, and someone much bigger than me knocks me down and steals the money, I will feel *sorrow*. If I get some more money and make my way back to the store, and while I am walking along I see the same thief staring at me from across the street, I may feel *fear*. If I make it to the store and offer my money to the clerk, and am told I need more than that to buy the apple, I may feel *anger* and *courageously* start to argue with the clerk, pointing out that, according to the price tag, I have the right amount.

This is a simple profile of human emotions, a good starting place for reflection on how God wants us to integrate emotions fully into our relationship with him.

S

Questions for Personal Reflection and Group Discussion

1. What idea in this chapter struck you most and why?

2. On a day-to-day basis, what role do your emotions tend to play in your activities and relationships? What is your habitual attitude toward feelings and emotions in general?

3. Try to remember specific instances in which you have felt each of the nine basic emotions. What triggered those feelings? How did you respond to them?

4. When your heart is in the right place, when you truly want, as your deepest desire, to grow in communion with God, you are better able to bring harmony into the often chaotic flurry of your emotions. For example, someone whose heart is set on winning a highly competitive scholarship may enter a severe crisis of circumstantial depression if he loses the competition. It may take months for this individual to recover an emotional balance and a healthy optimism about life. Someone else might compete for the same scholarship but see it merely as one excellent way to develop his or her talents so as to put them at the service of God and neighbor (the central desire of his or her heart) and thus will recover much more quickly from the disappointment of not winning the competition. What will you do today to allow your desire for God to shape and order your emotional world?

   - I will take some time this evening to talk with God in prayer about the high point and low point of the day, sharing my feelings with him and allowing his loving wisdom to temper them.
   - I will read Matthew 26 and list all the emotions that Jesus might have been feeling during those dramatic events. I will watch to see how Jesus reacts to those emotions and try to learn from that.
   - The next time I experience intense pleasure or joy, I will share it immediately with God by saying a prayer of thanksgiving.
   - (Write your own resolution) I will______________________________.

Concluding Prayer

Lord, I desire that in all things your will be done, because it is your will, and I desire that all things be done in the manner that you will them. Grant that I may always esteem whatsoever is pleasing to you, despise what you abhor, avoid what you forbid, and do what you command. I beg you to enlighten my understanding, to inflame my will, to purify my body, and to sanctify my soul.

My God, give me strength to atone for my sins, to overcome my temptations, to subdue my passions, and to acquire the virtues proper to my state of life. Fill my heart with tender affection for your goodness, hatred of my faults, love for my neighbor, and contempt of the world. May your grace help me to be obedient to my superiors, kind and courteous to my inferiors, faithful to my friends, and charitable to my enemies. Assist me to overcome sensuality by self-sacrifice, avarice by almsdeeds, anger by meekness, and carelessness by devotion.

My God, make me prudent in my undertakings, courageous in danger, patient in trials, and humble in success.

—from Pope Clement XI's Universal Prayer[13]

13 http://www.ourcatholicprayers.com/universal-prayer.html.

Chapter 13
Emotions in a Fallen World

In the Christian plan human beings are called to union with God as their last end, in whom they find their proper fulfillment, although they are impeded in the achievement of their vocation by the resistance which arises from their own concupiscence [selfish, unruly desires and tendencies].
—St. John Paul II, Address to Roman Rota, February 5, 1987

THE NINE BASIC emotions are just the raw material for this complex, powerful, and intriguing dimension of the human soul—the dimension of our feelings. The varied reality of day-to-day experience rarely stirs up any single one of them with perfect purity and clarity. Rather, they get mixed together in potent, and sometimes disturbing, combinations that include innumerable variations of intensity and hue. Life is simply too rich and multifaceted to fit neatly into predictable and easily manageable emotional boxes. Jesus alluded to this when he advised us to try to rise to the challenge of each day without fretting over vain attempts to control the bigger picture: "Do not worry about tomorrow; tomorrow will take care of itself. Sufficient for a day is its own evil" (Matthew 6:34).

The Variability of Emotions

The intensity of feelings will depend on just how significantly we judge that the stimulating object will promote or inhibit what is good for us. The greater the good or the more threatening the evil, the more intense the emotion: someone on the verge of winning a million dollars, for example, will usually feel more intense anticipation than someone on the verge of winning five dollars. Likewise, the specific quality or character of the object will give the basic emotion different flavors or levels of appeal or repugnance. The attraction of a beloved person, for example, will feel wildly different than the attraction of a good night's sleep. Objects can even both attract and repel us at the same time, under different aspects. Such is the complexity of the human experience.

Variations in external objects are not the only factors affecting our emotional world. Sometimes emotions seem to surge up from within, not responding to external stimuli at all, but preconditioning how we respond to those stimuli. These passionate emotional impulses are sometimes simply referred to as the "passions of the soul." Moods, for example, can color our emotional reactions, tainting with dejection what should objectively be hope-filled, or intensifying anger beyond what the situation truly deserves.

Moods and other internal influences can flow from simple biological processes—from hormonal fluctuation or indigestion or exhaustion, for example. But they can also have their roots in subconscious emotional patterns linked to past experiences. In a fallen world, no one escapes trauma of some kind or another. No one grows up with perfect parents and a perfectly balanced personality. The internal and external harmony that God built into creation was shattered by original sin. The journey to human maturity necessarily involves facing and coping with our own confusing internal divisions (what theologians call concupiscence) and with pain caused by the sins of those around us. Even before we are fully aware of ourselves and the world, our coping mechanisms are already conditioning the way we experience and handle emotions, and this conditioning is not always healthy for the long run.

The Purpose of Emotions

All this wonderful complexity helps explain why navigating our feelings is often so difficult. Yet it doesn't change the basic purpose of feelings, a purpose invented by God and built into our human nature. Knowing this purpose frees us to engage our feelings in our Christian adventure, not simply to suppress them.

Emotions construct a bridge between the outside, material world and our inner, spiritual world. As human beings, we are both spiritual and material. Our spiritual vocation to know and love what is true and good is given to us and unfolds in this material world. Our access to a greater knowledge and love of God is through our experience of this world. Our senses put us in contact with the realities around us, our intelligence and our will are meant to interpret those realities, and our emotions are meant to give us the energy we need to act in this world, to pursue what is good and avoid what is evil. Here's how the *Catechism* explains it:

> *Feelings or passions are emotions or movements of the sensitive appetite that incline us to act or not to act in regard to something felt or imagined to be good or evil.... The passions are natural components of the human psyche; they form the passageway and ensure the connection between the life of the senses and the life of the mind. (CCC, 1763–1764)*

Angels, as purely spiritual beings, have direct access to spiritual realities. They are emotionless. They don't laugh, and they don't cry. Their soul is intelligent, but solely spiritual—not nutritive (like the souls of plants) and not sensitive (like the souls of animals). They are moved to action by the pure and immediate perception of the objects they may choose. But we are not angels. Our access to the spiritual realities that alone will fulfill our yearning for happiness (infinite truth and infinite goodness) is given through the mediation of this material world. Our emotional reactions are meant to give us the fuel we need to pursue what is good and true and to resist what is evil and false.

The Unruliness of Emotions

Yet, unfortunately, in our fallen human nature this feeling function has been damaged. Our natural emotional reactions to the world around us are not in perfect harmony with God's plan for our full spiritual maturity. This is why our emotional experience so often seems to contribute to the stresses that plague the human predicament.

Our feelings often seem to have a mind of their own, independent of what we know to be true by reason or by faith. At times, for example, I feel drawn to things that my conscience deems wrong and damaging but my emotions deem desirable (like sleeping in when I have important work to do, or spending money that I don't have just to keep up appearances). At other times, I feel repulsed by things that my reason or my faith tells me are good and important but my emotions label as undesirable (like taking time out of my busy schedule to simply sit with the Lord and pray, or making a difficult but necessary phone call).

At still other times, the intensity of my emotions seems to have no basis in reality, and my moods swing wildly up and down, making life turbulent and chaotic (as when I take out my internal frustrations on someone I love, someone who has nothing to do with the real cause of those frustrations).

Yet, in spite of being so complex by nature and so off-kilter because of original sin, emotions remain an essential element of the human experience, and as such, they are a crucial factor in growing to spiritual maturity. This is why Jesus singled them out, commanding us to learn "to love the Lord your God with…all your soul" (Luke 10:27, RSV).

S

Questions for Personal Reflection or Group Discussion

1. What idea in this chapter struck you most and why?

2. What situations tend to trigger in you disproportionate emotional reactions?

3. In the past week, when have you experienced a clash between what you *felt* like doing and what you knew in your conscience that you *should* do? How did you react and why?

4. The first step in learning to better integrate our emotions into our love for God is to become more aware of the emotions that we feel. Some elements in our post-modern, consumer society don't want this to happen, because if we become more conscious of our emotional worlds,

we will be less vulnerable to emotional manipulation by insidious types of advertising. What will you do today to become more aware of how your emotions affect your decisions and behavior?

- After a conversation, I will take a few moments of silence to reflect on what I was feeling during the conversation, and the real reasons behind what I said and how I reacted.
- At the end of the day, I will think about how I used my free time and money during the day—what I occupied myself with and what I bought. Then I will reflect on *why* I made the decisions I did regarding free time and money, and how those decisions made me feel.
- (Write your own resolution) I will____________________________.

Concluding Prayer

May he support us all the day long,
till the shades lengthen and the evening comes,
and the busy world is hushed,
and the fever of life is over,
and our work is done.
Then in his mercy may he give us a safe lodging,
and a holy rest
and peace at the last.

—Blessed John Henry Cardinal Newman[14]

14 http://www.catholicity.com/prayer/prayers-and-hymns-by-john-henry-cardinal-newman.html.

Chapter 14
Forming My Emotions

To follow in every instance a "real" emotional impulse by invoking a love "liberated" from all conditionings, means nothing more than to make the individual a slave to those human instincts which St. Thomas calls "passions of the soul."

—St. John Paul II, Letter to Families, 14

THE PAINFUL AND complex disconnect between where our emotions often do pull us and where they ought to pull us is an undeniable aspect of life in a fallen world. We are made for God and for authentic good, and that is our deepest yearning, but our wounded human nature is easily distracted and deceived, and it often leads us astray.

St. Paul diagnosed this condition simply by reflecting on his own experience of internal division between our fallen nature and our redeemed nature:

> *For I know that good does not dwell in me, that is, in my flesh. The willing is ready at hand, but doing the good is not. For I do not do the good I want, but I do the evil I do not want… For I take delight in the law of God, in my inner self, but I see in my members another principle at war with the law of my mind. (Romans 7:18–19, 22–23)*

This is the human soul, an arena so often full of strife. This is the soul with which Jesus commands us to love God.

The Education of Emotions

The bottom line is simply that our capacity for these rich human experiences needs to be educated—and it can be educated! Under the Holy Spirit's guidance, we can bring our emotional potential into deeper and deeper harmony with what is true, good, and beautiful, so that our feeling function better fulfills its real purpose: energizing us in the pursuit of God's kingdom. This formation passes through three basic phases, which correspond to the three traditional stages of the spiritual life: the *purgative* way, the *illuminative* way, and the *unitive* way.

Purifying Our Emotions

In the first stage of spiritual growth, the *purgative* (or purifying) stage, our emotions need discipline. Like spoiled children who throw violent tantrums whenever their slightest whim is denied, undisciplined emotions tyrannically and violently seek to be indulged. But this is unhealthy. If we let our volatile emotional states and reactions dictate our behavior, we will stay spiritual infants forever.

A young wild horse has magnificent strength, great potential. But maximizing that potential requires training the horse to respond to the mind and will of its rider. The horse needs to learn how to carry a saddle, follow the reins, and recognize its rider's signals. In this way, the horse's raw strength can be harnessed for productive, fulfilling work.

Our emotions are kind of like that. They are a magnificent potential source of energy that can help our spiritual faculties flourish and lead us toward maturity and fulfillment. But they must learn docility to those higher faculties. And the first step in that process is holding them back from overindulgence by disciplining them. We simply can't let them run our lives if we truly want to live life to the full.

Integrating Our Emotions

Too often Christians stop the formation of emotions there, at the level of discipline and self-denial. But that is an incomplete view of the role of feelings. The purgative way is only the first stage. Discipline creates parameters for full freedom, but it is not the equivalent of full freedom. When that wild horse learns to sit still under tight rein, it is learning discipline. But unless it is also taught to walk and run without tossing its rider, the discipline will not have achieved its full purpose.

In the second stage of the spiritual life, therefore, God invites and helps us to move beyond seeing our emotions as the enemy of spiritual progress. Now that we are not enslaved to their every whim, we can learn to value them and understand them more deeply. We can face our own emotional wounds and coping mechanisms; we can give ourselves permission to feel our feelings deeply without fearing that they will sabotage us by always leading to sin. The horse is learning to run with and for its rider; our emotional world is expanding and making its powerful contribution to our pursuit of holiness, not just standing still with blinders on.

In this *illuminative* phase we learn the difference between life-giving emotional discipline and deadening emotional repression. God also gradually reveals to us the depth of our emotional needs, and he shows us how we can meet those needs in healthy ways, without reverting to the dangerous self-absorption of emotional immaturity. As our emotions thus truly become integrated into our relationship with God and our mission of building up his kingdom, our personality matures in harmony with our growing faith, and we become stable, content, joyful Christians.

Perfect Harmony

As our feelings enter more and more into the service of the truths of faith that are meant to govern our lives, as God teaches us to feel our feelings without letting them dictate our decisions, our emotional world gradually comes into almost perfect sync with our authentic good. This is what our feelings look like in the *unitive* way.

Emotionally mature Christians feel not only a *spiritual* attraction to prayer and the sacraments and works of mercy, but also an *emotional* resonance with those and similar God-centered activities. Their feelings have learned to perceive a truly good object in actions that used to be emotionally dry.

Likewise, as our emotions are fully integrated with our faith, we find ourselves spontaneously repulsed by spiritually dangerous objects that used to appear attractive. The prospect of a shady but lucrative financial deal can be an agonizingly seductive temptation for someone still in the purgative stage. But when our emotions have been formed by faith and conformed to Christ's own authentic desires for what is truly good and not just apparently good, an invitation to obvious material sin often elicits an emotional revulsion, regardless of the monetary benefits that it may proffer.

Our Destination

This was the experience of so many saints and martyrs—mature Christians who have cooperated generously with God's grace and found themselves desiring with their whole being whatever God desired for them, even if it was a cross. And the most comforting thing of all is that those saints and martyrs started out just like us, fallen and wounded and spiritually immature. The grand partnership of God's grace and their generous effort slowly but surely transformed them, just as it will do for us. Here's how St. Paul described it, showing us that discipline (being crucified with Christ) led him to a mature faith (illuminative way) and an indescribable union of mutual love with the Lord. This is where God is leading all of us—to love him with all our soul:

> *I have been crucified with Christ; yet I live, no longer I, but Christ lives in me; insofar as I now live in the flesh, I live by faith in the Son of God who has loved me and given himself up for me.* (Galatians 2:19–20)

At the beginning of our journey, and sometimes in the middle of it, St. Paul's words may not resonate with us—the discomfort caused by a feeling function in need of formation still predominates. But God is at work there, and every sacrifice and every small step we take at his side toward spiritual maturity will yield wildly disproportionate fruits: "Draw near to God, and he will draw near to you" (James 4:8).

S

Questions for Personal Reflection or Group Discussion

1. What idea in this chapter struck you most and why?

2. How fully are your emotions integrated into your life of faith? (Keep in

mind that different sectors of your emotional experience can have different levels of integration.) How often, for example, does the prospect of obeying your conscience even when it's tough energize you instead of paralyzing you? Or how often do you go to prayer (personal prayer, Sunday Mass) only out of dry duty as opposed to out of duty bolstered by a real, emotionally felt desire?

3. Which of your emotional reactions need to be better disciplined? Which need to be more fully integrated into your relationship with God?

4. So many great pieces of music have been written out of faith in and devotion to God. And music is one of the main stimulants of emotion. This shows us, once again, that even though our emotional world is often hard to manage, it's something that God really wants to redeem. What will you do today to better harness the great potential of your emotions for the good of your life's mission?

    - I will sincerely express my affection to my spouse or another family member, rather than taking them for granted.
    - I will plan ahead this week, so as to be able to take time on Sunday, the Lord's Day, to really enjoy God's gifts and celebrate his goodness.
    - (Write your own resolution) I will_____________________________.

Concluding Prayer

O my God! I offer you all my actions of this day for the intentions and for the glory of the Sacred Heart of Jesus. I desire to sanctify every beat of my heart, my every thought, my simplest works, by uniting them to its infinite merits; and I wish to make reparation for my sins by casting them into the furnace of its merciful love. O my God! I ask of you for myself and for those whom I hold dear, the grace to fulfill perfectly your holy will, to accept for love of you the joys and sorrows of this passing life, so that we may one day be united together in heaven for all eternity.

—A Morning Offering written by St. Thérèse of Lisieux[15]

15 https://www.ewtn.com/Devotionals/prayers/therese3.htm.

Part IV
Loving God with All My Mind

On the last and greatest day of the feast, Jesus stood up and exclaimed, "Let anyone who thirsts come to me and drink. Whoever believes in me, as scripture says: 'Rivers of living water will flow from within him.'" He said this in reference to the Spirit that those who came to believe in him were to receive. There was, of course, no Spirit yet, because Jesus had not yet been glorified.... Jesus spoke to them again, saying, "I am the light of the world. Whoever follows me will not walk in darkness, but will have the light of life." (John 7:37–39; 8:12)

Chapter 15
Following the Light

My special hope for you is this: that you will always have a great love for truth—the truth about God, the truth about man and the truth about the world. I pray that through truth you will serve humanity and experience real freedom. In the words of Jesus Christ: "You will know the truth and the truth will set you free" (John 8:32).

—St. John Paul II, Address, September 11, 1987

EMOTIONS PROVIDE THE energy we need to take action in life. But they need to be educated so they can move us toward actions that truly contribute to what is best for us and for the world around us. The wild horse needs to be taught to obey its wise rider.

That rider may want to go in the right direction—his or her *heart* may be in the right place. But what if the rider simply doesn't know the way to get there? What if the rider's intelligence lacks the necessary knowledge and light and capacity to recognize the proper landmarks and follow the true path? In that case, it will be impossible to make progress. This is why our Lord singled out this capacity of the human person when he gave us the great commandment: "You shall love the Lord your God...with *all your mind*" (Mark 12:30, emphasis added).

A Darkened Mind

Original sin ruptured the original harmony that God had built into the human family's relationship with himself, with the created world, and with each other. It also wounded human nature from within, including our spiritual faculties (intelligence and will). Before the Fall, our first parents saw and grasped clearly God's plan for themselves and for the world. They saw things as God saw them.

Then, after the Fall, humanity became "subject to ignorance," as the *Catechism* puts it (*CCC*, 405). The world became a place full of shadows and threats. God became distant and mysterious, and religion degenerated, in most cases, into fear-inspired superstition. The human person became a puzzle to himself; the true meaning of human life, our origin, our purpose, and our path to achieve that purpose, became shrouded in darkness. Mankind became lost in a labyrinth of confusion that our own rebellion against God had constructed. St. Paul reveals the starkness of the situation, commenting on the persistent wickedness of a fallen race:

> *For although they knew God they did not accord him glory as God or give him thanks. Instead, they became vain in their reasoning, and their senseless minds were darkened. While claiming to be wise, they became fools and exchanged the glory of the immortal God for the likeness of an image of mortal man or of birds or of four-legged animals or of snakes. Therefore, God handed them over to impurity through the lusts of their hearts for the mutual degradation of their bodies. They exchanged the truth of God for a lie and revered and worshiped the creature rather than the creator, who is blessed forever. Amen.* (Romans 1:21–25)

The Coming of the Light

An essential ingredient in God's plan for redeeming such a benighted human family, therefore, was light—the light of truth. The story of salvation includes a gradual, gentle, and glorious revelation of the truth about God, the world, and ourselves. This revelation began immediately after the fall of our first parents, continued and developed throughout the history of the Old Covenant, and reached its culmination in the incarnation, life, passion, death, and resurrection of Jesus Christ.

The New Covenant in Jesus, also known as the New Testament, explains and brings to fulfillment all that went before in the Old Testament. In Christ, we have been given new access to the truth that our minds were created to discover, explore, and grasp. We have been shown a sure path out of the deadening ignorance that forms part of the inheritance of sin: "I am the light of the world," Jesus proclaimed (and he certainly proclaimed it with a beaming and inviting smile, not with a fierce and ferocious frown); "whoever follows me will not walk in darkness, but will have the light of life" (John 8:12).

The Deepest Questions

Who are we? Where do we come from? What is our purpose? What will make us truly happy? Why is there evil in the world? How can we live life to the full? What happens after death? How are we supposed to deal with the challenges and sufferings of life?

Mankind has posed these questions throughout its turbulent history. They are the basic questions of the human mind, because they respond to the fundamental human need and desire to know the truth—not just a few individual truths, like the laws of physics and the contents of our neighbor's cupboards, but the truth, the way things are. Until we know that, or at least some key elements of it, we cannot be completely free to flourish as God means us to; our minds remain unfulfilled, groping in the dark.

Since human nature is always the same, these questions are always the same. Every epoch, every culture, every religion has to face them. We are compelled by our own nature to answer these questions somehow, for the good of our minds, just as we are compelled by our own nature to find food and shelter for the good of our bodies.

The Fullest Answer

This is the real reason why the different religions seem so similar when they are looked at from certain perspectives: They all seek to give answers to the same basic questions that come with our fallen human nature. And some of the answers that the different religions and philosophies offer contain shards of the truth, because our minds are made to find truth, and we can indeed find some truth through sincere searching. St. Paul also made this point in his discussion about the wickedness of idolatry:

> *For what can be known about God is evident to them, because God made it evident to them. Ever since the creation of the world, his invisible attributes of eternal power and divinity have been able to be understood and perceived in what he has made. As a result, they have no excuse. (Romans 1:19–20)*

And yet, if our own efforts were sufficient, Jesus would never have had to come to give us his revelation. Only in that revelation do we have access to the fullness of truth that we crave and are created for, the truth that will free us from darkness and allow us to live life abundantly, now and for all eternity:

> *Jesus then said to those Jews who believed in him, "If you remain in my word, you will truly be my disciples, and you will know the truth, and the truth will set you free." (John 8:31–32)*

As the *Catechism* instructs us, human reason unaided by the light of revelation will always remain, at some level, frustrated:

> *In the historical conditions in which he finds himself, however, man experiences many difficulties in coming to know God by the light of reason alone.... This is why man stands in need of being enlightened by God's revelation.* (CCC, 37–38)

Learning to love God with all our mind—coming to know, understand, and accept deeply all that he has revealed to us about himself, ourselves, and the world—is the path out of that frustration. We cannot truly seek God's kingdom without following it.

S

Questions for Personal Reflection or Group Discussion

1. What idea in this chapter struck you most and why?

2. Recall the time in your life when you first began to ask deeper questions. Are you still hungry for the truth that will set you free? Why or why not?

3. How well do you know the truths that God has revealed to you through Christ? Have you ever tried to explain the gospel to someone who hasn't heard it yet? If not, would you be able to do so?

4. St. Dominic, the medieval founder of the Dominican Order of Preachers, required a radical poverty from his first members. They weren't allowed to own anything at all, either individually or corporately. They were to travel by foot, spreading the gospel. The only exception to their extreme austerity was books. He wanted all his men to be able to take their books with them wherever they went so they could constantly renew and deepen their knowledge of God's saving Word. What will you do today to deepen your knowledge of God's revelation?

    - I will make a list of questions I have about the faith and then make an appointment to talk to a priest or expert about them.
    - I will read the testimony of a non-Catholic who converted to Catholicism. (A resource for such testimonies is The Coming Home Network, www.chnetwork.org/converts.)
    - (Write your own resolution) I will__________________________.

Concluding Prayer

Creator of all things, true source of light and wisdom, lofty origin of all being, graciously let a ray of your brilliance penetrate into the darkness of my understanding and take from me the double darkness in which I have been born, an obscurity of both sin and ignorance. Give me a sharp sense of understanding, a retentive memory, and the ability to grasp things correctly and fundamentally. Grant me the talent of being exact in my explanations, and the ability to express myself with thoroughness and charm. Point out the beginning, direct the progress, and help in completion; through Christ our Lord. Amen.

—St. Thomas Aquinas[16]

16 http://www.catholicdoors.com/prayers/english/p00404.htm.

Chapter 16
Where to Seek the Truth

The Church wishes to serve this single end: that each person may be able to find Christ, in order that Christ may walk with each person the path of life, with the power of the truth about man and the world that is contained in the mystery of the Incarnation and the Redemption, and with the power of the love that is radiated by that truth.
—St. John Paul II, *Redemptor Hominis,* 13

HEALTHY CHRISTIANS EXPERIENCE an avid yearning to learn more about God and how to live more and more in communion with him, just as healthy babies experience a driving hunger for the food that will enable them to grow. In different seasons of life, however, and for different reasons, the yearning itself can diminish, or we can silence it by focusing on less taxing or seemingly more practical aspects of following Christ. We need to keep an eye out for that. Loving God with all our minds means constantly seeking to get to know him better. When our knowledge of him becomes stale, our love too will become stale.

We live in a fallen world, and growing in spiritual maturity requires intentionally swimming against that fallen world's current. As soon as we stop, worldliness carries us backwards. This is why St. Paul encouraged the Christians in Rome, who had already received the gift of faith and the Holy Spirit, to continue seeking the renewal of their minds:

> *Do not conform yourselves to this age but be transformed by the renewal of your mind, that you may discern what is the will of God, what is good and pleasing and perfect.* (Romans 12:2)

Finding Food

In past ages, getting access to the message of Christ often required heroic efforts. Copies of the Bible were few, precious, and highly protected. And the vast majority of the population lacked enough education to be able to read the sacred Scriptures even if they had been more widely available. The faith was passed on largely through preaching and teaching, through the liturgical celebrations and the liturgical calendar (which often dictated the civil calendar), through the witness of consecrated men and women, and through local traditions. Even in difficult circumstances, however, God is still God, and the Holy Spirit has always found ways to instruct those who choose to make seeking a deeper knowledge of Christ and his kingdom a high priority—every era has its saints.

In post-modern times, the situation is different. Instead of a shortage of information, we have a glut of it. We are caught in a lava flow of information. We could spend all our waking hours reading, listening to, and watching the billions and billions of bytes that form the fluid and multimedia Internet library at our fingertips. Our problem isn't *finding* sources that can deepen our knowledge of God and his revelation; our problem is *choosing* which ones to use, and following through with the decision to use them.

Whom to Listen to

The most important criterion to follow as we make those choices is Christ's own: "Whoever listens to you listens to me. Whoever rejects you rejects me" (Luke 10:16). Jesus has given to the world a teacher authorized to speak in his name, and he has promised to protect that teacher from error in all things regarding faith (what God has revealed about himself, his creation, and his plan of salvation) and morals (what God has revealed about how we must live in order to reach spiritual maturity). This teacher is his Church, the preserver and explainer of the gospel message as it comes to us, especially through sacred Scripture (the Bible) and sacred tradition (everything else the apostles received through the Holy Spirit and passed on to the Church).

The Church's authentic teaching office is called her Magisterium, and its dependability is guaranteed through the Holy Spirit's guidance of Christ's vicar on earth, the pope, and the bishops who teach in communion with him. As members of the Church, we all share in what theologians call the *sensus fidei,* or "supernatural sense of faith," by which revelation is maintained and understood down through the ages, but the Magisterium has a special role to play in that process. Here is how the *Catechism* explains it:

> *In order to preserve the Church in the purity of the faith handed on by the apostles, Christ who is the Truth willed to confer on her a share in his own infallibility. By a "supernatural sense of faith" the People of God, under the guidance of the Church's living Magisterium, "unfailingly adheres to this faith."* (CCC, 889)

As we actively seek to expand and deepen our knowledge of God and his plan of salvation, the Magisterium provides clear reference points, firm anchors, and healthy parameters around which we can freely and confidently grow in our knowledge of the truth. These come primarily in the form of instructions from popes and bishops (such as encyclicals and the *Catechism*) and are explained by dependable Catholic sources (homilies, books, articles) that apply them to the different circumstances of life. Without those reference points, anchors, and parameters, we would return to the hesitant, fearful exploration that characterizes so many Christ-less paradigms. Without them, we could easily fall into seductive but destructive errors—for example, the heresies that have caused so many wounds throughout the centuries, the post-modern rationalizations of abortion and euthanasia, or even the false ideologies that have justified such horrific crimes as the Nazi holocaust and the Soviet gulags.

We need to stay humble and accept God's truth. We need to allow the Church to be for us, as it was for St. Paul, "the household of God, which is the church of the living God, the pillar and foundation of truth" (1 Timothy 3:15).

Fearless Pursuit of Truth

This doesn't mean that a good Christian is only permitted to read the Bible, the *Catechism*, and papal encyclicals—not at all. God draws each of us into a unique relationship with him. This uniqueness will be reflected in our individual journey of knowing God better. But whatever patterns emerge as we journey along the renewal of our mind, certain basic vitamins must never be depleted; we have to give ourselves daily doses of dependable truth, regular intellectual meals that only come with intentional and conscientious study of our authentically Catholic faith.

We have to gradually master the basic truths of revelation so we can recognize when they are contradicted or threatened by other ideas we run across. We have to continue developing our understanding of the implications of those basic truths so we cultivate the capacity to make mature and truthful judgments in tough situations. We have to seek greater familiarity with Christ's message so we can, as St. Peter put it, "always be ready to give an explanation to anyone who asks you for a reason for your hope, but… with gentleness and reverence" (1 Peter 3:15–16).

And finally, we need to continually increase our knowledge about God, correcting any false ideas we may have about him and expanding our grasp of the truth about him so we can continually increase our love for and dedication to God. We cannot love what we do not know, and we cannot love more deeply what we know only superficially. Jesus came to earth to be our light, to roll back the suffocating darkness of ignorance and sin through his unique message of salvation. Loving him with all our minds means filling them, more and more every day, with that light:

> *Moreover, we possess the prophetic message that is altogether reliable. You will do well to be attentive to it, as to a lamp shining in a dark place, until day dawns and the morning star rises in your hearts. (2 Peter 1:19)*

S

Questions for Personal Reflection or Group Discussion

1. What idea in this chapter struck you most and why?

2. How much time and effort do you currently put into getting to know your faith better and better?

3. When it comes to being informed about current issues and events from

the point of view of the Magisterium, would you describe yourself as proactive or reactive? Why?

4. Very few of us are able to study our faith full-time. God understands this. But we do manage to find time every day to study something—we watch the news or our favorite TV series; we visit our favorite websites; we fill our minds with knowledge about things we are interested in. Daily learning more about our faith can happen in the same, natural, unexaggerated way. What will you do on a daily/weekly basis to learn something new about the "inscrutable riches of Christ" (Ephesians 3:8)?

    - I will attend an adult faith-formation event at my parish.
    - I will attend a public lecture or guest-speaker event at a nearby Catholic college or university.
    - I will search for a good Catholic website and sign up to receive daily or weekly e-mail updates.
    - (Write your own resolution) I will__________________________.

Concluding Prayer

O Lord my God, I believe in you, Father, Son and Holy Spirit. Insofar as I can, insofar as you have given me the power, I have sought you. I became weary and I labored. O Lord my God, my sole hope, help me to believe and never to cease seeking you. Grant that I may always and ardently seek out your countenance. Give me the strength to seek you, for you help me to find you and you have more and more given me the hope of finding you. Here I am before you with my firmness and my infirmity. Preserve the first and heal the second. Here I am before you with my strength and my ignorance. Where you have opened the door to me, welcome me at the entrance; where you have closed the door to me, open to my cry; enable me to remember you, to understand you, and to love you.

—St. Augustine of Hippo[17]

17 Prayer to Seek God Continually, Villanova University Mission & Ministry, http://www1.villanova.edu/villanova/mission/campusministry/spirituality/resources/spirituality/restlesshearts/prayers.html.

Chapter 17
More Than Information

This, then, is the marvelous yet demanding task awaiting all the lay faithful and all Christians at every moment: to grow always in the knowledge of the richness of baptism and faith as well as to live it more fully.
—St. John Paul II, *Christifideles Laici,* 58

CHRISTIANIZING THE MIND, learning to love God with our whole mind, involves more than simply filling our heads with information. The mind is more than a hard drive. The human mind, our intellect, is a directive power built into our nature. Our capacity to know shows us the way things are and the way we should behave. To value and form these capacities in harmony with our Christian vocation requires taking some time to reflect on their various dimensions. As we show and grow our love for Christ in this arena of our lives, we need to be aware of at least three things, three interrelated functions of the human mind: information gathering, thinking deeply, and training our memory.

Gathering Information

Though information gathering—learning, coming to know more both in breadth and depth—is not the only function of the mind, it is a primary function. The healthy desire for more knowledge about our faith, and about how to live out that faith, flows from this function. A steady increase of knowledge is necessary for spiritual growth. Jesus is the Word of God, and a word communicates content, meaning. The more we know about

God, about God's purpose for the world, about God's plan of salvation, and about how God sees us and wants to interact with and guide us, the better.

Receiving God's revelation and grasping it with our minds overcomes the natural ignorance of our human condition. It also gradually purifies us of the malicious misinformation that we imbibe by living in a fallen world with a fallen nature. We are full of distorted ideas about ourselves, our world, and God. God's revelation is given to us to expose these lies and enlighten our darkened intellects.

Thirsting for deeper knowledge of our beloved Lord is a common theme in the Scriptures. The Psalmist puts it succinctly: "Blessed are you, O Lord; teach me your statutes" (Psalm 119:12). The Book of Proverbs repeats it untiringly:

> *Hear, O children, a father's instruction, be attentive, that you may gain understanding! Yes, excellent advice I give you; my teaching do not forsake.... The beginning of wisdom is: get wisdom; whatever else you get, get understanding. (Proverbs 4:1–2, 7)*

A healthy Christian is, among other things, a *learning* Christian.

Going Deeper

The second function of the intellect has to do not so much with gathering more and more information, but rather with deepening our understanding of the truths we already know and thinking deeply about them. A schoolboy can memorize the Gettysburg Address, but the words he memorizes will mean much less to him than they did to Abraham Lincoln when he wrote that address. Truth has breadth, but it also has depth.

The Latin root for the word *intelligence* includes two words: *intus* and *legere*. Together they connote "reading into" something—penetrating the deeper meaning of things. Our minds are meant to do this, too. When we forget about this, we may grow in breadth of knowledge, but we will not necessarily grow in wisdom, in understanding. We will be like a computer with lots of data, but not necessarily a deeper spiritual person, in tune with the true meaning of God's wonderful universe.

One of the Blessed Virgin Mary's traditional titles is "Seat of Wisdom." In the New Testament she models this dimension of the human mind, this quest not just for breadth but for depth. Multiple times, the Gospels show her mulling over, intentionally and prayerfully, God's revelation in Christ: "And Mary kept all these things, reflecting on them in her heart" (Luke 2:19).

Remembering

The third function of our intellect links our minds (a spiritual power) to our memories (a sensitive power). Loving God with our whole mind involves training our memory so that it easily retrieves whichever ideas, impressions, or experiences will help us most in each stage of our spiritual journey.

In order to interact with the world around us in a Christian way, we have to learn to recall the truths of revelation and allow them to guide and enlighten us in the various life situations we encounter. What good is it to be able to define Divine Mercy if we refuse to allow that mercy to give us hope and comfort after we commit a grievous sin?

Ancient Israel had a memory problem. God would perform amazing miracles for them, and a week later, when things got tough, they would forget about the miracles and stir up a tempest of whining and complaining. They would also forget about God's action in their lives in times of prosperity, slipping into a comfortable self-sufficiency that led them to neglect their relationship with him.

The temptation to forget about God's faithfulness and presence is a strong one. God vehemently warned Israel about it in the Old Testament: "Be careful not to forget the Lord, your God…" (Deuteronomy 8:11). The entire chapter expands on this warning. We see the same warning in the Book of Revelation. In Revelation chapters 2 and 3, Jesus issues a series of reprimands and encouragements to the seven churches of Asia. In each one of them, he chastises or commends the members of the community in terms of what they have forgotten or kept in mind, what they have held onto or what they have lost. And his indications about how the churches should move forward usually include a reference to repenting and remembering, to persevering along the path that they took up at the beginning. Here is how he exhorts the church in Sardis, for example:

> Remember *then how you accepted and heard;* keep it, *and repent. If you are not watchful, I will come like a thief, and you will never know at what hour I will come upon you.* (*Revelation 3:3, emphasis added*)

Keeping the truths of our faith constantly in sight so that we remain faithful to our calling in spite of the failures and successes, the sufferings and temptations that necessarily go along with life in a fallen world—this, too, is the job of a mind that seeks to love the Lord.

Imagining

Connected to this capacity for memory is the power of imagination, another bridge between the sensitive and spiritual powers of our soul. Our imagination allows us to picture in our mind's eye good things or bad things, noble things or base things. When we are feeling sad, for example, we can allow our minds to wander over to memories of even sadder situations or concoct images of how things could get worse. This would increase our sadness. On the other hand, we could also harness this power of our mind to help us rekindle hope, by picturing the crucifixion and the resurrection, for example, or by picturing the Sacred Heart of Jesus—the pledge of his undying love for us.

Our imagination can enhance all the other intellectual functions: gathering and learning information, penetrating the depths of the truths we learn, and recalling those truths in order to allow them to influence our daily living. But for this to happen, we have to educate and develop the imagination. Unfortunately, this training is severely handicapped by consumerism (which keeps our imaginations dependent and reactive so advertising images can be used to manipulate our emotions) and by media saturation (which keeps our imagination overloaded and therefore almost uncontrollably frenetic).

We need to recognize that the Christianization of our intellects involves developing harmoniously all these facets of our minds. A Christian mind is a mind that has learned God's revelation, assimilated it, and taken ownership of it. As a result, mature Christians will naturally see themselves, others, the world, events, and God through the clear window of truth. But reaching that maturity requires a daily decision to love the Lord with all our minds, actively seeking to grow in Christian knowledge and godly wisdom, the wisdom that addresses itself to us through the sacred Word:

> *Happy the one who listens to me, attending daily at my gates, keeping watch at my doorposts; for whoever finds me finds life, and wins favor from the LORD; but those who pass me by do violence to themselves; all who hate me love death.* (Proverbs 8:34–36)

S

Questions for Personal Reflection or Group Discussion

1. What idea in this chapter struck you most and why?

2. Which do you tend to like more, gathering new knowledge or going deeper with the knowledge you already have? How can you achieve a better balance between these two complementary tendencies?

3. To form your memory and imagination, you have to be aware of them. How conscious are you, on a day-to-day basis, of what your memory and imagination are up to? How docile are they to your will?

4. St. John of the Cross, the sixteenth-century Spanish mystic and doctor of the Church, would very often spend large chunks of time simply gazing out his window at the beauties of God's creation. By contemplating God's works in this way, he absorbed God's wisdom and filled his mind with its light. What will you do today to grow in godly wisdom?

    - I will have a good conversation with a friend about how our faith sheds light on a major current event.
    - I will read my favorite Gospel passage, and then close my eyes and try to picture it—in every detail—in my imagination.
    - I will make a list of ten of the biggest blessings I have received throughout my life, remembering and savoring them.
    - (Write your own resolution) I will________________________________.

Concluding Prayer

O Mary, Mother of fair love, of fear, of knowledge, and of holy hope, by whose loving care and intercession many, otherwise poor in intellect, have wonderfully advanced in knowledge and in holiness, you do I choose as the guide and patroness of my studies; and I humbly implore, through the deep tenderness of your maternal love, and especially through that eternal Wisdom who deigned to take from you our flesh and who gifted you beyond all the saints with heavenly light, that you would obtain for me by your intercession the grace of the Holy Spirit that I may be able to grasp with strong intellect, retain in memory, proclaim by word and deed, and teach others all things which bring honor to you and to your Son, and which for me and for others are salutary for eternal life. Amen.

—St. Thomas Aquinas[18]

18 http://www.ourcatholicprayers.com/prayers-before-studying.html.

Chapter 18
Leveraging the Power of Literature and Art

Every piece of art, be it religious or secular, be it a painting, a sculpture, a poem or any form of handicraft made by loving skill, is a sign, a symbol, of the inscrutable secret of human existence, of man's origin and destiny, of the meaning of his life and work. It speaks to us of the meaning of birth and death, of the greatness of man.
—St. John Paul II, Address at Clonmacnoise, Ireland, 1979

INFORMING AND FORMING our intellectual power is essential for learning to love God with our whole mind. Yet none of our human faculties exists in a vacuum—we can't really Christianize our mind without that having an indirect positive effect on our emotions and our will, as well as our heart. This is especially the case with regards to one specific intellectual pursuit, which at first glance doesn't even seem to be particularly relevant for our relationship with God: appreciating the fine arts, especially literature.

Not everyone loves literature, and certainly not every saint has been steeped in literary masterpieces. In fact, plenty of saints have reached the heights of holiness without even knowing how to read. And so, no one needs to feel obliged to utilize great literature as a means for spiritual growth. Yet it is a tested tool—a resource tried and proven, again and again, to enrich the human spirit. Understanding how the intelligent enjoyment of literature does that can give us another instrument to help us learn to love God with all our minds. Something similar can be said for all the fine arts, but since literature is the most accessible and all-embracing, we will focus our discussion here.

What Is Literature?

The literary arts include poetry, fiction, and drama, though some would add history to the list. Literature has come to be understood as a written art form, although the first great epics all originated as oral traditions, and the great dramas only really come to life when they are performed. From the earliest times, recited poetry and performed dramas also included musical elements. The literary arts, then, overlap with the other performing arts.

Because of this overlap, defining the different forms of literature can be problematic. But for the sake of discussing the role of literature in the spiritual life, we can identify certain defining characteristics.

All forms of literature give intelligible shape to what we experience in our human journey. They help us process our experience; they help us understand ourselves and our world; they help us move beyond what is superficial and live at the level of significance. They also give us joy. The beauty of good literature brings the disparate elements of our busy and demanding lives into a pleasing and inspiring harmony, reminding us of our true identity, our true potential, and our true destiny as creatures made in the image and likeness of God. This beauty also nourishes our heart by feeding good, true desires for the source of all beauty, goodness, and truth—God himself. Each form of literature achieves these noble goals in its own way.

The Magnifying Power of Poetry

Poetry, whether oral or written, tends to be more concise than prose. A poem will focus our attention on a detail of our human experience and delve into its meaning. Imagery and careful choice of words and rhythms give poetry its power to uncover the beauty and significance of every nuance of the human condition. Poetry encourages calm reflection on and appreciation of each precious piece of the mosaic of human experience.

The application of poetry to the spiritual life, then, is obvious. Mental prayer, whether meditative or contemplative, involves deep reflection on God and his goodness. It creates space in the soul for the truth and beauty of God to shine on our minds and hearts. Poetry complements meditation. By revealing the deeper meaning hidden within the details of human experience, it sensitizes us to God's ubiquitous presence. It teaches us to read the first book of God's revelation—the created world.

The Motivating Dynamism of Drama

In drama, the emphasis is on virtue: the power of the human spirit to seek and seize what is good. Good dramas—whether on stage or screen—show protagonists exercising their freedom, sometimes heroically, to avoid and conquer evil in pursuit of authentic happiness. Conflict, whether internal or external, is the core of drama. When sin and evil defeat the hero, we have a tragedy. When the hero overcomes sin and evil, we have a triumph. Both tragedies and triumphs have their place in our journeys.

Literary genius appears in drama through the author's capacity to include just the right amount and quality of events, conversations, and decisions, such that the audience feels deeply both the attraction of goodness and the threatening or seductive tug of evil. As the drama unfolds, the audience experiences vicariously the struggle of the protagonist. The better the drama, the deeper the identification between the audience and the protagonist, and it is according to the depth of that identification that the tragedy or the triumph will inspire audience members to repent of their own sins and to renew their hope-filled pursuit of what is true, good, and beautiful. Drama, then, can refresh, encourage, reinforce, or rekindle our good desires—an invaluable contribution indeed to our spiritual lives.

The Interior Landscape of Fiction

The unique characteristic of fiction is the interior monologue. The great novels are almost poetic in their descriptions of the world and of human experience. They also involve the dramatic struggle between good and evil. But their specific contribution is opening a window into the human psyche. Tolstoy can spend a dozen pages describing a single moment of psychological experience: the mixed motives, the subconscious influences, the conflicting feelings, the waning or waxing hopes, and the nudging of conscience that are present in a person's interior at any given moment in life's journey. Through an author's description of what is happening inside the human person, readers get to know the characters much more profoundly than in a drama. And when the characters are developed truly, in consonance with our authentic identity as fallen and redeemed spiritual persons, this knowledge enriches us in two important ways.

First, it helps us reflect on and get to know ourselves better. The great literary authors are like expert psychologists: Their works are a mirror in which we are enabled to see parts of our own interiors that we normally cannot fathom. Second, it helps us understand other people and their experiences. We walk in their shoes for a while, and this vicarious experience can, if we let it, empower our efforts to be merciful, forgiving, understanding, compassionate, and supportive toward our neighbors.

Just a Means—Not the Goal

The other fine arts, like music, painting, and sculpture, can have a similar positive effect on our spiritual development, if we have the time and opportunity to learn their language. Of course, the realm of the arts poses spiritual dangers, too: False values can be paraded in attractive disguises; connoisseurship can devolve into snobbery; and entertainment can overrule edification. But all in all, an intelligent and prudent engagement with humanity's artistic achievements will be a boost for thinking about "whatever is true, whatever is honorable, whatever is just, whatever is pure, whatever is lovely, whatever is gracious" (Philippians 4:8, RSV).

S

Questions for Personal Reflection or Group Discussion

1. What idea in this chapter struck you most and why?

2. What stories (in whatever form—book, film, drama) have most inspired and influenced you over the years, and why?

3. Through the ages, the Church has been a consistent and avid patron of the arts. Why is that?

4. What will you do today to open yourself more to benefit from the human family's artistic treasures?

    - I will listen to a favorite piece of classical music.
    - I will start reading one of the classics that I have always wanted to read.
    - I will take some time to observe and admire the religious art present in my parish church.
    - (Write your own resolution) I will____________________________.

Concluding Prayer

Lord, you are the hope of your people.
You give artists the gift of reflecting your splendor in their work;
Through the things they make, make the world bright with hope and joy.

—From the Liturgy of the Hours

Chapter 19
Spiritual Gluttony

The situation today points to an ever-increasing urgency for a doctrinal formation of the lay faithful, not simply in a better understanding which is natural to faith's dynamism but also in enabling them to "give a reason for their hoping" (1 Peter 3:15) in view of the world and its grave and complex problems.

—St. John Paul II, *Christifideles Laici,* 60

THE DESIRE TO learn more about our faith is a good one, a godly one, a desire planted and tended by the Holy Spirit. It leads us to engage our intellect, memory, and imagination in the quest to love God with our whole mind.

For some Christians, the need to know more, to learn more, to "think of what is above, not of what is on earth" (Colossians 3:2), often feels like a burden. These Christians have to wage a constant battle against the sin of spiritual sloth—laziness when it comes to things of the spiritual life.

But for other Christians, the drive to expand and deepen our knowledge of God and his revelation provides not only supernatural benefits, but also natural pleasure. In some cases, it can stir up temptations to spiritual gluttony—a less obvious, and therefore more dangerous, arena of sin.

Keeping Tabs on Frustration

God is infinite, so we will never come to know him so fully that nothing remains to discover. And yet sometimes we rebel against that reality. We become frustrated because we can't find more time to study and learn, to master everything there is to master about our faith, or about certain aspects of our faith. We yearn to learn more and more, but we run into so many obstacles: time limits, energy limits, resource limits. Even the basic responsibilities of our state in life seem to be obstacles in our going deeper with God, and so we begin to neglect them. All our free time, all our conversations, all our friendships—all our everything becomes more and more stuffed with devotions, and spiritual talks, and Bible studies, and faith-sharing groups, and conferences, and retreats, and seminars. And even then, we are frustrated because we can't fit more in.

This frustration seems holy, because it is directed toward wanting to know God better. But something deeper is going on. This is clear, because instead of leading us to greater internal peace and external generosity, the flurry of spiritual over-consumption seems to make us tense, anxious, brittle, and even judgmental. What's really happening?

Frustrations of this kind are dangerous traps along our spiritual journey, traps often set by the ancient enemy, the devil himself. Christians thirsting for more knowledge of the faith are too in love with God to be exceptionally vulnerable to temptations of *material* excess. So the devil has to change tactics in order to impede their spiritual progress. Enter spiritual and intellectual gluttony. If our spiritual and intellectual eyes get bigger than our stomachs, and we act on that, we will experience some spiritual indigestion, and that will become a nice ally in the devil's efforts to slow our progress along the path of Christian maturity.

Spiritualizing the Capital Sins

Both sloth and gluttony are capital sins—sins that give rise to other sins. We are used to seeing them in the material sphere, but we are not so used to seeing what they look like when they are spiritualized; yet sooner or later these sins do indeed show up on the doorstep of faithful, maturing Christians, dressed up in their spiritual disguises.

We experience pleasure in learning about the God we love. This is a good thing—all pleasures, in their proper settings, are good things. God created both our capacity for pleasure and the objects that stimulate those pleasures. The devil can't change that. But he can twist it around a bit, and he can get us to be more and more attached to the pleasure to the point that we begin preferring the pleasure itself—in practice if not in theory—to the God who created it.

We understand this clearly in the material realm. The physical pleasures associated with gluttony, lust, and sloth are obvious. We are less aware of the spiritualized forms of these capital sins. If our eagerness to learn about God and our faith stirs up anxiety, tension, conflict, and frustration instead of contentment and joyful enthusiasm, some intellectual gluttony may be creeping in. When this happens, we need to nip it in the bud. We need to accept once again, intentionally, the truth that we already know: We will never be able to learn everything about God and the spiritual life; our journey to Christian maturity will continually present new vistas and discoveries, and we don't have to try to exhaust them.

The Right Amount

The practical trick for keeping our God-given desire for greater knowledge healthy is to think in terms of the next step. We don't need to look at the 3.3 million volumes in the libraries at the great Catholic universities. Rather, we should look at the two or three books (or whatever other resources) that we really feel drawn to right now and dip into them, working through them and seeking to increase both the breadth and the depth of our knowledge. As we work through these books, other titles will come onto the radar screen. Put them on a wish list. When we are ready for another book, we can look through the list and see which ones draw us most intensely. This is often how the Holy Spirit guides us. He will draw us to certain titles or classes or other resources, and we will find ourselves just kind of following along. He knows what will help us most in each moment and each season of our journey, and he often guides us in subtle, gentle ways.

Another practical approach, for those who like planning and organizing, is to set some personal study goals for each liturgical season, or for each calendar year. Plan ahead what you would like to study, thinking through it intentionally, and then get all the materials, place them on your active bookshelf, and work through them gradually, enjoyably, peacefully.

You might have a goal, for instance, of reading three books on prayer this winter, or reading all the works of St. Francis de Sales this year. As more items and ideas pop up, put them on your wish list and pile them onto your inactive bookshelf. This approach can be used as an individual, or by plugging into study circles with other fellow Christian travelers.

Grateful Trust

We should be grateful for the good, holy desire that we feel deep inside—the desire to know better and better all that God has revealed to us about himself, this world, and the way to live our lives to the full. We need to continue acting on this desire, but doing so with the childlike humility and joy that Jesus values so much. We will always have more to discover as we venture toward the Father's house, and that should fill our hearts with delight, not frustration.

S

Questions for Personal Reflection or Group Discussion

1. What idea in this chapter struck you most and why?

2. Are you more tempted to spiritual sloth or spiritual gluttony?

3. How intentional are you in your efforts to continually renew your mind in Christ? How intentional should you be, and what would that look like in your daily life?

4. While she was on her deathbed, the medieval queen, St. Elizabeth of Hungary, talked with her visitors about all the best spiritual sermons and homilies she had heard during her life. This shows that she had been eager to learn more about her beloved God, but that she had also taken enough time to digest what she heard. What will you do today to improve this area of your Christian living?

    - I will think about what tends to frustrate me, and try to discover why I get frustrated about those things.
    - I will make a list of the types of things I tend to be slothful about, and the types of things I tend to be gluttonous about. I will choose

one thing from each list to improve on this week.

- I will make a realistic personal reading list for the next couple of months.
- (Write your own resolution) I will________________________________.

Concluding Prayer

All holy Father, eternal God, in your goodness you prepared a royal throne for your Wisdom in the womb of the Blessed Virgin Mary; bathe your Church in the radiance of your life-giving Word, that, pressing forward on its pilgrim way in the light of your truth, it may come to the joy of a perfect knowledge of your love. Grant this through our Lord Jesus Christ, your Son, who lives and reigns with you and the Holy Spirit, one God, forever and ever. Amen.

—Collect from the Mass of Our Lady, Seat of Wisdom

PART V

Loving God with All My Strength

As they were proceeding on their journey someone said to him, "I will follow you wherever you go." Jesus answered him, "Foxes have dens and birds of the sky have nests, but the Son of Man has nowhere to rest his head." And to another he said, "Follow me." But he replied, "[Lord,] let me go first and bury my father." But he answered him, "Let the dead bury their dead. But you, go and proclaim the kingdom of God." And another said, "I will follow you, Lord, but first let me say farewell to my family at home." [To him] Jesus said, "No one who sets a hand to the plow and looks to what was left behind is fit for the kingdom of God." (Luke 9:57–62)

Chapter 20
The Strength to Decide

Called to salvation through faith in Jesus Christ, "the true light that enlightens everyone" (John 1:9), people become "light in the Lord" and "children of light" (Ephesians 5:8), and are made holy by "obedience to the truth" (1 Peter 1:22).

—St. John Paul II, *Veritatis Splendor,* 1

BY LOVING GOD with all our mind, we open ourselves to receive light and guidance about the right path to take through life. Our intellect is bathed in and nourished by the truth of God's revelation, and the ignorance and confusion we inherited from original sin is gradually corrected and purified. But *knowing* something is not the same as *doing* something.

The intellect is not the only spiritual power in human nature. We also have the power of free choice, of decision: The human intellect and the human will must work together, under the light of faith and the strengthening of grace, in order to move us forward on the path of spiritual maturity. We must know the truth more and more deeply, but we also must freely choose to act in accordance with the truth we know, and we must make that choice repeatedly, day after day, situation after situation. The wild horse of our soul must have a rider that both knows where to go and is fully determined to get there. To grow in our love for God, then, includes loving him not only with all our mind and all our soul, but also with all our *strength*.

The Sad Young Man

The Gospels relate a memorable encounter that vividly illustrates how a weak will can impede spiritual progress. A rich and godly young man had heard about Jesus, the wonder-working rabbi from Nazareth. He had heard enough to come to believe in him, to believe that Jesus had the answers that his soul yearned for. And so, he went out to seek the Lord.

When he found him, he was so excited and eager that he "ran up, knelt down before him, and asked him, 'Good teacher, what must I do to inherit eternal life?'" (Mark 10:17). This was the right question! He wanted to know the deeper truth, and he believed Jesus could reveal it to him. His mind was open to the light.

Jesus recognized this and engaged in a conversation with him. He first told him to follow the commandments, since those were the path to fulfillment built right into human nature. But the young man replied that he was faithful to the commandments, and he wanted to know what else was missing, because he felt that his heart was still empty in some way. Again, we see that his mind was open to the light of truth; his conscience was making solid judgments and pushing him toward deeper immersion in God's revelation.

At that point, Jesus, "looking at him, loved him and said to him, 'You are lacking in one thing. Go, sell what you have, and give to [the] poor and you will have treasure in heaven; then come, follow me'" (Mark 10:21). Jesus gave him the answer. Jesus revealed to this sincere and well-instructed young man what was holding him back: an inordinate attachment to his wealth, and to the comfort and the apparent self-sufficiency that wealth brings. Jesus showed him the true path to deeper communion with God. The young man now knew the truth about how he could take the next step toward spiritual maturity.

In the man's response to this illumination, the Scriptures reveal the most common obstacle to spiritual growth, a weak will, a will enervated by inordinate attachments. St. Mark describes how the young man reacted to the answer he had been so avidly seeking: "At that statement his face fell, and he went away sad, for he had many possessions" (Mark 10:22). This man's capacity to choose the true good, his freedom—the precious gift we receive in order to enable us to love consciously and dynamically what is good, as persons, and not simply to follow unconscious instincts, like the rest of the animals—was hampered. He was not free to follow the higher good, the good he knew and desired, because his will was enchained, at least in part, to a lesser good.

The True and the Good

Jesus always linked knowledge of the truth with action in accordance with that knowledge. In his conversations with the Jewish leaders of his time, as well as his conversations with his own disciples, he repeatedly emphasized this connection. It is not enough to know and believe God's truth in the abstract; we must also choose to act and live in harmony with our faith—otherwise our union with God is impaired, and our wills remain divided and separated from God's will. And in fact, even knowledge of God's revelation remains immature without a growing obedience to that revelation:

> *Jesus answered them and said, "My teaching is not my own but is from the one who sent me. Whoever chooses to do his will shall know whether my teaching is from God or whether I speak on my own." (John 7:16–17)*

The spiritual life, as Jesus has revealed it, consists not merely of some secret or magical knowledge, as many non-Christian religions and heresies have asserted through the centuries. Rather, the spiritual life, the life of grace and growth in holiness, is an interpersonal relationship. More than just learning about God, it involves getting to know God. And getting to know someone means walking with them and living at their side, not only sharing common knowledge, but sharing *life* with them, being united in thought as well as in will, in both our spiritual faculties.

Jesus himself made this starkly, even frighteningly, clear at the end of his Sermon on the Mount. After pouring out his instruction, his light, his revelation regarding God and regarding the path to true happiness, he wraps things up with a stern warning against being satisfied with a mere knowledge *about* those things without advancing, through obedience, to a knowledge *of* them:

> *Not everyone who says to me, "Lord, Lord," will enter the kingdom of heaven, but only the one who does the will of my Father in heaven. Many will say to me on that day, "Lord, Lord, did we not prophesy in your name? Did we not drive out demons in your name? Did we not do mighty deeds in your name?" Then I will declare to them solemnly, "I never knew you. Depart from me, you evildoers." (Matthew 7:21–23)*

The bridge between knowing and doing is built only by the spiritual power of our will. Engaging this power in our relationship with God is how we come to love him with all our strength. At this point, you may be wondering how you can do this better. That's what the following chapters will cover.

S

Questions for Personal Reflection or Group Discussion

1. What idea in this chapter struck you most and why?

2. Can you think of any inordinate attachments in your life, now or in the past, that have shackled or limited your freedom?

3. Jesus said, "Amen, amen, I say to you, everyone who commits sin is a slave of sin" (John 8:34). What do you think he meant? How is this relevant to your own spiritual journey right now?

4. St. Teresa of Avila, the sixteenth-century Spanish foundress and doctor of the Church, used to say that an eagle could be kept from flying either by chaining it to the ground, or simply tying it there with a little string. It's important for us to be humble and honest in our self-examination about what might be holding us back in our spiritual journey, so that God's grace can really get to work. Take some time to ask Jesus in prayer to show you, as he showed the rich young man in Mark 10, what is lacking in your efforts to follow him more closely. At the end of the day, take some more time to reflect on what he showed you, and then renew your commitment to "do whatever he tells you" (John 2:5).

- I will take some time to sit alone with God and ask him what the rich young man asked him: "Lord, what must I do to keep growing in my relationship with you?" Prayerfully reflecting on this question, I will write down all the things that come to mind.
- I will consciously look for an opportunity today to do a good deed, a deed that fulfills, even in a small way, the commandment, "Love your neighbor as yourself" (Mark 12:31).
- I will look at my list of daily duties each day this week and start with the least enjoyable item, the one I would rather put off til later. I will offer this as a sacrifice to God, uniting it to Christ's redeeming cross through a little prayer.
- (Write your own resolution) I will______________________.

Concluding Prayer

O Mary,
Mother of Mercy,
watch over all people,
that the Cross of Christ
may not be emptied of its power,
that man may not stray
from the path of the good
or become blind to sin,
but may put his hope ever more fully in God
who is "rich in mercy" (Ephesians 2:4).
May he carry out the good works prepared
by God beforehand (see Ephesians 2:10)
and so live completely
"for the praise of his glory" (Ephesians 1:12).

—St. John Paul II[19]

19 *Veritatis Splendor*, 120.

Chapter 21
Building Well

Revelation teaches that the power to decide what is good and what is evil does not belong to man, but to God alone. Man is certainly free, inasmuch as he can understand and accept God's commands. And he possesses an extremely far-reaching freedom, since he can eat "of every tree of the garden." But his freedom is not unlimited: it must halt before the "tree of the knowledge of good and evil" (Genesis 2:16–17), for it is called to accept the moral law given by God. In fact, human freedom finds its authentic and complete fulfillment precisely in the acceptance of that law. God, who alone is good, knows perfectly what is good for man, and by virtue of his very love proposes this good to man in the commandments.

—St. John Paul II, *Veritatis Splendor,* 35

MANY POST-MODERN ideologies and theories of human behavior tend to either over- or underemphasize the power of human freedom. These have seeped into popular culture at every level, and in some cases they have even affected how we understand the gospel itself.

A Dangerous Disconnect

Behaviorist and immanentist schools of thought tend to blame all of our behaviors and choices on influences beyond our control. According to them, subconscious or unconscious complexes and urges or circumstantial and social pressures exercise so much influence on a person's decisions that moral responsibility disappears. Some secularist and relativistic schools of thought, on the other hand, see the human mind as all-powerful. For them, not only can we freely determine what we choose to do, we can also freely and independently determine the very nature of good and evil.

Both of those errors shatter the link between freedom and truth, between truth and goodness. If the human person is completely determined by urges and circumstances, then our dignity disappears, as does our capacity for spiritual creativity, friendship, loyalty, love, and any other moral virtue that would give authentic meaning to life. If, on the other hand, the human person is actually divine, unlimited in our capacity to create meaning and truth simply by willing to do so, then every individual becomes, in essence, a universe unto himself, and the possibility of true communion between persons (human and divine) disappears. In either case, the theoretical divorce between truth and goodness is a lie that, if accepted, makes interior peace, fulfillment, and authentic happiness impossible.

Jesus Believes in Us

Jesus freed us from these lies. In the first place, he acknowledged and accepted the complex influences that contribute to conditioning our freedom in this fallen world. This is why he commanded us not to judge the interior intentions and culpability of other people—we simply cannot know enough to make a full and accurate judgment about a person, even when a particular action is objectively wrong. Only God sees clearly the many circumstantial and subconscious influences that may be at work inside a person's soul. It is enough for us to seek light regarding our own soul, without trying to manage the souls of others:

> *Stop judging, that you may not be judged. For as you judge, so will you be judged, and the measure with which you measure will be measured out to you. Why do you notice the splinter in your brother's eye, but do not perceive the wooden beam in your own eye? How can you say to your brother, 'Let me remove that splinter from your eye,' while the wooden beam is in your eye? You hypocrite, remove the wooden beam from your eye first; then you will see clearly to remove the splinter from your brother's eye.* (Matthew 7:1–5)

Our Lord, however, never exaggerated the role of external influences. He always believed in us. He always appealed to our spiritual ability to make good choices, to exercise our freedom in harmony with the truth, and in that way to achieve the maturity, wisdom, and holiness that we are created for.

Yet he didn't fall into the other trap either. He never exaggerated the power of our freedom, exonerating us from the duty to humbly obey the truth. We are called not to be gods, but to love God, and that includes following God's plan for the human family in general, and for our individual life in particular. This conscious, free obedience to the truth promotes the fulfillment of our highest spiritual potential, and it alone leads to the meaning, fruitfulness, and happiness that will last. His respect for our capacity to do what is right and true, his hope in us, shines through in the finale of the Sermon on the Mount, a passage we have already seen:

> *Everyone who listens to these words of mine and acts on them will be like a wise man who built his house on rock. The rain fell, the floods came, and the winds blew and buffeted the house. But it did not collapse; it had been set solidly on rock. And everyone who listens to these words of mine but does not act on them will be like a fool who built his house on sand. The rain fell, the floods came, and the winds blew and buffeted the house. And it collapsed and was completely ruined. (Matthew 7:24–27)*

The True and the Good

The same tone of exhortation fills the pages of the entire New Testament. In Christ, with him and through the gift of his grace, each of us has become "a new creation: the old things have passed away; behold, new things have come" (2 Corinthians 5:17). As a result, if we remain in the Lord and stay united to the vine, our collaboration with God's grace can truly work wonders in us and through us: "I am the vine, you are the branches. Whoever remains in me and I in him will bear much fruit, because without me you can do nothing" (John 15:5).

We *can* learn to love God with all our strength. We *can* choose to follow Christ and travel the path of spiritual maturity. We *can* resist temptation and grow in virtue. We *can* make a difference in the world, building Christ's kingdom and encouraging others to do the same. If we couldn't, none of the New Testament letters would have been written, since they all contain passionate encouragement to make practical, daily choices worthy of our Christian calling. If knowing the truth were sufficient for our spiritual growth, and if we were not free to choose to live according to that truth, St. Paul, for example, would never have written this:

> *Put to death, then, the parts of you that are earthly: immorality, impurity, passion, evil desire, and the greed that is idolatry.... Put on then, as God's chosen ones, holy and beloved, heartfelt compassion, kindness, humility, gentleness, and patience, bearing with one another and forgiving one another, if one has a grievance against another; as the Lord has forgiven you, so must you also do. And over all these put on love, that is, the bond of perfection.... And whatever you do, in word or in deed, do everything in the name of the Lord Jesus, giving thanks to God the Father through him.* (Colossians 3:5, 12–14, 17)

When our hearts desire God above all things, and our emotions are joyfully subject to an intellect enlightened by faith and a will strengthened and aligned by grace, we can truly love God with all our heart, soul, mind, and strength, just as Jesus commands.

S

Questions for Personal Reflection or Group Discussion

1. What idea in this chapter struck you most and why?

2. What is your knee-jerk reaction to the concept of "obedience"? Where does that reaction come from?

3. In what kinds of situations do you feel more acutely the temptation to accept the lie that truth and freedom are enemies instead of co-principles of spiritual maturity?

4. A visitor once asked Blessed Mother Teresa of Calcutta what he could

really do to help the poor, since he felt so small and un-influential. She answered, "Pick up a broom." What will you do today to obey Jesus better by putting your freedom at the service of the truth, to be a better "co-worker in the truth"? (3 John 8).

- I will make a good examination of conscience and go to confession.
- I will think about my own persistent unhealthy behavior patterns and try to figure out where their roots are. Then I will think of what kind of behaviors I could develop to correct those unhealthy patterns. I will talk to God about it and ask for his help.
- I will read the explanation of the Ten Commandments in the *Catechism*.
- (Write your own resolution) I will________________________.

Concluding Prayer

O Lord and Master of my life,
Grant not unto me a spirit of idleness,
of discouragement,
of lust for power,
and of vain speaking.
But bestow upon me, Thy servant,
the spirit of chastity,
of meekness,
of patience,
and of love.
Yea, O Lord and King,
grant that I may perceive
my own transgressions,
and judge not my brother,
for blessed art Thou
unto ages of ages.
Amen.
—St. Ephrem the Syrian[20]

20 http://www.stjohnchrysostom.org/OurTraditions/Prayers/CommonPrayers.aspx.

Chapter 22
Persevering

At no stage of life can people feel so secure and committed that they do not need to give careful attention to ensuring perseverance in faithfulness; just as there is no age at which a person has completely achieved maturity.
—St. John Paul II, *Vita Consecrata,* 69

IT'S ONE THING to make good choices, to use our freedom to grow in love, as we are called to do, rather than forfeiting our freedom to the slavery of attachments and sin. But the power of the human will isn't exhausted by only choosing to follow the right path in isolated moments. Loving God with all our strength also means persevering on that path. Our Lord left no room for doubt on this: "But the one who perseveres to the end will be saved" (Matthew 24:13). And just to make sure we understand, he illustrated this fundamental truth with a visual metaphor: "No one who sets a hand to the plow and looks to what was left behind is fit for the kingdom of God" (Luke 9:62).

Levels of Maturity

Babies are immature; their will is undeveloped, just as are many other of their natural powers. They have no conscious awareness or control over their emotions, their whims, their passions, and their drives. Their spiritual freedom is in an embryonic state: They are completely dependent on the care and education of others. Just as they need to be potty-trained, they also need to be feelings-trained; they need to learn how to integrate their passions into a harmonious, mature personality under the guidance of their intelligence and their will. In the meantime, they are overly swayed by the pleasure and whim of the moment, by their biorhythms and their moods.

Adolescents are usually more mature. They can make independent, creative plans, and they can follow through on them, if they like them and feel the immediate rewards—just think of how much dedication a boy can put into mastering a video game. The will has grown and developed and can be directed toward achievements that take time and perseverance. But adolescents usually remain inordinately attached to immediate gratification, to easy pleasure. Even physiologically, certain areas of the brain that enable more mature judgment are still developing until we reach our twenties. The will, too, is still developing, and still needs training. This is why it is often so hard for adolescents to persevere in tasks where the reward is distant or in jobs that they simply don't enjoy. They need help to discipline themselves in those areas where they feel less immediate gratification and where overindulgence in pleasure can cause them moral or emotional damage.

The adolescent may or may not show up to fulfill his commitments. He will begin grand projects on a whim, in the wake of an emotional high, and then leave them half-finished. The adolescent can make excellent and numerous resolutions for personal, academic, extracurricular, or spiritual improvement. But those resolutions will quickly fizzle out, and they will be replaced by another set of resolutions, which will also fizzle out, and the pattern continues. This is the activity of a will that is still immature. A person with an immature will *would like* to do many worthy things, but in actual practice, the "I would like" may never upgrade itself to the full, mature "I will."

Mature adults have developed the capacity for self-governance. They are able to navigate the ebb and flow of emotional energy and maintain a steady, determined pace in pursuit of worthy goals. They are responsible, dependable, and persevering. Without denying their real and legitimate needs for healthy pleasure and gratification, mature adults are able to keep their internal stature ordered and secure, so as to continue worthwhile pursuits over the long haul. They are able to envision how much effort certain commitments or objectives will take, and so they make their decisions with sufficient reflection, knowing what will be required of them. They are committed enough to follow through even though it will be costly, because they have maturely judged (intellect) and maturely decided (will) that the endeavor is worthwhile.

The Cost of Discipleship

Jesus described this steadiness, this healthy realism, this capacity of perseverance, with two of his vivid parables. He emphasized how essential mature willpower—a will liberated from inordinate attachments that inhibit the freedom to love fully (renouncing all possessions)—really is for Christian discipleship:

> *Which of you wishing to construct a tower does not first sit down and calculate the cost to see if there is enough for its completion? Otherwise, after laying the foundation and finding himself unable to finish the work, the onlookers should laugh at him and say, "This one began to build but did not have the resources to finish." Or what king marching into battle would not first sit down and decide whether with ten thousand troops he can successfully oppose another king advancing upon him with twenty thousand troops? But if not, while he is still far away, he will send a delegation to ask for peace terms. In the same way, every one of you who does not renounce all his possessions cannot be my disciple.* (Luke 14:28–33)

It is possible to have reached adulthood physiologically and to still be an infant or an adolescent as regards the maturity of one's will. In this case, even full-grown, worldly, successful adults may be unable to love God as much as they really want to, because a lot of that strength is simply not yet available to them; in some senses, they are still babies. But growth in this area can happen very quickly, once we plug in to God's grace and make a firm decision to follow him more closely each day. (We will look more into how to do that in the last part of this book.)

It is also possible to be a child or an adolescent physiologically and have already developed a relatively mature will. But maturity doesn't mean that love has reached its limit. As the mind and soul continue to grow in "wisdom and in stature, and in favor before God and man," the "all" of a person's love for God will also continue to grow (Luke 2:52, RSV).

Whatever our current level of spiritual maturity, we do well to remember that love is intrinsically dynamic, and it will always have room to keep on expanding. Obeying the command to love God with all our strength, therefore, is a lifetime project.

S

Questions for Personal Reflection or Group Discussion

1. What idea in this chapter struck you most and why?

2. In which areas or relationships of your life do you still lack maturity or interior freedom?

3. What life experiences have helped you the most along your path of becoming more mature, responsible, and dependable as a person? How and why did those experiences help you so much?

4. Strengthening your will is much easier to do than you might think. Willpower is like a muscle, and the more we exercise it, the more it grows. The key is to exercise it with faith and prayer, so that we always stay under the light of God's grace and never start thinking we can simply achieve spiritual maturity by trying harder. What will you do today to strengthen your will in loving service of God's plan for your life?

    - I will follow through on a task or commitment that I have been procrastinating.
    - I will start my day by doing the least pleasant item on my to-do list, saving the more pleasing things for later (as a kind of reward).
    - I will make a weekly schedule around my most important priorities and then make a concerted effort to *follow that schedule,* saying "no" to nonessential, unplanned needs and opportunities that pop up.
    - (Write your own resolution) I will______________________________.

Concluding Prayer

I arise today,
through God's strength to pilot me;
God's might to uphold me,
God's wisdom to guide me,
God's eye to look before me,
God's ear to hear me,
God's word to speak for me,
God's hand to guard me,
God's way to lie before me,
God's shield to protect me,
God's hosts to save me
from snares of the devil,
from temptations of vices,
from every one who desires me ill,
afar and anear,
alone and in a crowd…
Amen.

—St. Patrick of Ireland[21]

21 http://www.worldprayers.org/archive/prayers/invocations/i_arise_today_through_a_mighty.html.

Chapter 23
This Present Darkness

For in spite of all the witness of creation and of the salvific economy inherent in it, the spirit of darkness is capable of showing God as an enemy of his own creature, and in the first place as an enemy of man, as a source of danger and threat to man. In this way Satan manages to sow in man's soul the seed of opposition to the one who "from the beginning" would be considered as man's enemy—and not as Father. Man is challenged to become the adversary of God!

—St. John Paul II, *Dominum et Vivificantem,* 38

SECULAR ATHEISTS CAN develop strong willpower and natural prudence, and they can put them to work in the service of impressive and useful achievements. They can develop the natural virtues of responsibility and dependability through persevering effort. But when we aim at serving God's kingdom instead of the kingdom of this world, an additional set of obstacles gets involved. The spiritual battle kicks in, a struggle, as St. Paul explains, that "is not with flesh and blood but with the principalities, with the powers, with the world rulers of this present darkness, with the evil spirits in the heavens" (Ephesians 6:12).

The Spiritual Struggle

Developing willpower always demands effort and sacrifice, but aligning our will with Christ's and growing in Christian courage and perseverance—which always require obedience, not just sheer determination—

will demand even more. Both our intellect and our will are wounded by original sin, as we have seen, and when we launch out on the path of healing and make loving obedience to God's plan the desire of our hearts, our spiritual enemies become intensely interested in deterring us. St. John Paul II explained this is in his encyclical on the moral life:

> *This obedience is not always easy. As a result of that mysterious original sin, committed at the prompting of Satan, the one who is "a liar and the father of lies" (John 8:44), man is constantly tempted to turn his gaze away from the living and true God in order to direct it towards idols (cf. 1 Thessalonians 1:9), exchanging "the truth about God for a lie" (Romans1:25). Man's capacity to know the truth is also darkened, and his will to submit to it is weakened. Thus, giving himself over to relativism and skepticism (cf. John 18:38), he goes off in search of an illusory freedom apart from truth itself.*[22]

The Enemy's First Strategy: Corrupt the Heart

Jesus had to fight this battle in his life, too. His nature wasn't wounded by original sin or personal sins, but he had to do combat with our ancient enemy, the devil. And in that combat, he revealed the devil's three basic strategies.

At the beginning of his public life, Jesus went into the desert wilderness for forty days for prayer and preparation. During that period, the Gospels explain, he was "tempted by Satan" (Mark 1:13). We are all familiar with the temptations that were used in this case (see Matthew 4). In these, the devil tried to divide Jesus's heart, in order to remove or at least corrupt his core desire of loving and obeying his Father. The devil tried to replace it with a desire for pleasure and comfort when he tempted our Lord to turn stones into bread. When that didn't work, the devil tried to replace it with a desire for earthly power and dominion, showing our Lord all the kingdoms of the world and promising to put them under his control for the simple price of worshipping the devil. That didn't work either. And so the devil tempted Jesus to seek first popularity and adulation by performing a dramatic miracle

22 St. John Paul II, *Veritatis Splendor*, 1.

of jumping off the top of the temple without being hurt. That temptation failed as well. The devil's first strategy, to corrupt the heart, was laid bare.

The Enemy's Second Strategy: Turn Aside the Will

St. Luke finishes his narration of the temptations in the wilderness by pointing out that "when the devil had finished every temptation, he departed from him for a time" (Luke 4:13). That time came to an end on the eve of our Lord's passion. After Jesus was betrayed, St. Luke tells us, the Lord explained that "the time for the power of darkness" had returned (Luke 22:53). During Jesus's passion, we learn about our enemy's other two strategies.

In the Garden of Gethsemane, the devil bombarded Jesus with temptations so deep that they inspired fear and confusion and caused him "sorrow and distress" (Matthew 26:37). So profound was the struggle that Jesus sweated blood (see Luke 22:44) and even exclaimed to his companions, "My soul is sorrowful even to death" (Matthew 26:38). For centuries, theologians have debated the exact nature of these temptations, but all agree that whatever their content (and this is where temptations try to corrupt the intellect, sowing false ideas or deceptive half-truths), their goal was clear: The devil was trying to get Jesus to disobey his Father's will, to say no to what his Father was asking of him. And this is the second strategy, to turn aside our will from God's will—to make God's will seem so unreasonable or painful or difficult that our courage fails, and we choose a different path.

The devil can't create reality; he is not God. And so he has to distort it in order to frighten us. To keep us from entering a path that God is inviting us to follow, he has to exaggerate the danger or the difficulty. We already know that it will be difficult, because Jesus revealed this to us:

> *Enter through the narrow gate; for the gate is wide and the road broad that leads to destruction, and those who enter through it are many. How narrow the gate and constricted the road that leads to life. And those who find it are few. (Matthew 7:13–14)*

But Jesus would never ask something of us that is absolutely impossible. This is what the devil wants to make us forget. He wants us to see God's invitation only from a human, mundane perspective. That is when our courage will likely fail. But God always reminds us that such a perspective is incomplete: "Jesus looked at them and said, 'For human beings this is impossible, but for God all things are possible'" (Matthew 19:26).

The Enemy's Third Strategy: Getting Us to Give Up

Jesus resisted the devil's onslaught in the Garden of Gethsemane, mainly through fervent prayer (see Luke 22:44). And so the enemy switched to his third basic tactic. He couldn't dislodge the Lord's heart, and he couldn't convince him not to set out on the path of the Father's will, so he made following that path agonizingly difficult. The passion and death of our Lord involved suffering betrayal, injustice, physical and psychological torture, humiliation, calumny, rejection of all types, and even witnessing heartrending sorrow in those whom he loved most, such as his Mother. Every step along the path of his Father's will increased his suffering. Every increase of suffering required a renewal of his loving obedience. The devil was simply trying to wear him out, trying to make him suffer so much that he would eventually rebel against his Father's plan and turn aside from the path he had freely chosen to follow—the right path, the path of loving God with all his heart, soul, mind, and strength. Continuing down that path required perseverance; it required mature human willpower, infused with and elevated by divine grace.

S

Questions for Personal Reflection or Group Discussion

1. What idea in this chapter struck you most and why?
2. How aware are you of the reality of spiritual warfare in the world and in your own life?
3. Consider the devil's three strategies in relation to the challenges you have faced or are facing now. Which of the strategies seems to be most effective in impeding your spiritual progress?

4. St. Maximilian Kolbe, a Franciscan priest, founder, and martyr of Auschwitz, used to tell his fellow Franciscans that he would be able to help them a lot more once he got to heaven. In heaven, he said, he could use both hands to help them. Here on earth, he could only use one hand, because he had to use the other hand to keep himself from falling. What will you do today to better unite yourself to Jesus and allow God's grace to strengthen you in the spiritual battle?

    - I will think prayerfully about the temptations that most typically trip me up. I will prayerfully come up with a practical way to respond courageously the next time that temptation appears.
    - I will memorize the prayer to St. Michael the Archangel (at the end of this chapter), and use it as a spiritual shield the next time I feel tempted.
    - I will read about how my patron saint engaged in spiritual battles and draw inspiration from his or her example.
    - (Write your own resolution) I will ______________________.

Concluding Prayer

St. Michael the Archangel,
defend us in battle.
Be our defense against the wickedness and snares of the Devil.
May God rebuke him, we humbly pray,
and do thou,
O Prince of the heavenly hosts,
by the power of God,
thrust into hell Satan,
and all the evil spirits,
who prowl about the world
seeking the ruin of souls. Amen.

—Pope Leo XIII[23]

23 http://www.ewtn.com/devotionals/prayers/michael.htm.

PART VI
Getting Practical

Come to me, all you who labor and are burdened, and I will give you rest. Take my yoke upon you and learn from me, for I am meek and humble of heart; and you will find rest for yourselves. For my yoke is easy, and my burden light. (Matthew 11:28–30)

Chapter 24
The Path of Life

Where can you turn to find answers that satisfy, answers that will last? The opposite of deception is truth—the person who tells the truth, the person who is the truth. Yes, the opposite of deception is Jesus Christ, who tells us: "I am the way, and the truth, and the life" (John 14:6). Jesus Christ is the Son of God. He reveals the truth of God. But he is also man. He shares in our humanity and came into the world to teach us about ourselves, to help us discover ourselves.

—St. John Paul II, Address to Young People, September 12, 1987

WHEN AN APPLE tree is mature, when its roots are firmly, deeply grounded in good soil with plenty of water, when its trunk is strong and healthy and protected by sturdy bark, when its branches are smooth and supple and covered with wide green leaves that drink in the sunlight, it blossoms and bears fruit. Its potential is being realized. It has grown in accordance with its nature and is glorifying God, reflecting a small ray of God's own goodness and beauty by being all that it was created to be. The innate powers of the tree are flourishing together harmoniously.

All the innate powers of the human person are enlisted by the Lord in his command to love God with "all your heart, with all your soul, with all your mind, and with all your strength" (Mark 12:30). When each of these powers is harmoniously integrated into the ongoing pursuit of greater union with God, which is the purpose of our existence, our potential is being realized, we are glorifying God, and the fruits of the Spirit are blossoming, ripening, and enriching our lives and the lives of those around us: "The fruit of the

Spirit is love, joy, peace, patience, kindness, generosity, faithfulness, gentleness, self-control" (Galatians 5:22–23). Those fruits of the Spirit have no limits. The more we are united to God, the more intense and abundant they become, as Jesus pointed out, and as we have previously noted: "I came so that they might have life and have it more abundantly" (John 10:10).

Growing in Virtue

Forming these powers so that they are directed in a healthy way, toward the truth and goodness that are in accordance with our nature and our calling, is what the Christian spiritual tradition calls growing in virtue. The virtuous person, from this long-standing perspective, is the one who is most alive, the one whose soul is most mature. Growing in virtue sets the human person free to be all that we were created to be, just as the healthy apple tree, when all its powers reach maturity, is free to fulfill its inherent potential.

Growing in virtue, then, is the same thing as growing in happiness. Just as an apple tree remains frustrated (ontologically, not consciously) if the soil or other conditions inhibit its roots and branches and leaves from growing to maturity, so human beings remain frustrated and unhappy when their hearts haven't discovered and desired to pursue their proper goal, when their intellects aren't being nourished on the eternal truths, when their wills aren't engaged in authentically meaningful and creative activity, and when their passions aren't enjoying docility to the spirit.

Only when we are on the path of learning to love God with all our heart, soul, mind, and strength—only when we are on the path of growing in virtue—do we experience the vitality, the hopefulness, the keen satisfaction that enables mature Christians to say such shocking things as St. Paul did:

> *[But] whatever gains I had, these I have come to consider a loss because of Christ. More than that, I even consider everything as a loss because of the supreme good of knowing Christ Jesus my Lord. For his sake I have accepted the loss of all things and I consider them so much rubbish, that I may gain Christ. (Philippians 3:7–8)*

As we move forward along the path of deeper union with God, the path of growing in virtue, our experience of the fulfillment that only God can give increases and intensifies, gradually obliterating all idols.

A Progressive Journey

Here on earth, we never reach the limit of that experience. Rather, God continues to present us with situations in which, if we so desire, our virtue can continue to grow and expand, thereby continuing to intensify our experience of keen inner vitality and clarity. We remain pilgrims, moving along through time and space toward our final destination in heaven, as long as we remain residents of earth. As Christian pilgrims in the world, we are "aliens and sojourners" (1 Peter 2:11), because "…here we have no lasting city, but we seek the one that is to come" (Hebrews 13:14). Yet every step of love that leads us closer to the eternal city also increases our union with God, matures our virtue, and enhances our vitality. No one is more alive than a saint.

So even as the circumstances in which we live continue to be marked by the pain, sorrow, and brokenness of this fallen world, our interior experience as we navigate those circumstances takes on more and more the flavor of holiness. We begin to understand, better and better, the peace that Jesus bequeathed to us during the Last Supper—an inner, overflowing peace that differs from any satisfaction available from the goods of this passing world: "Peace I leave with you; my peace I give to you. Not as the world gives do I give it to you. Do not let your hearts be troubled or afraid" (John 14:27). As we grow in virtue, we begin to understand how St. Paul, who was never trite or superficial or overly optimistic, was able to command Christians to rejoice at all times:

> *Rejoice in the Lord always. I shall say it again: rejoice! Your kindness should be known to all. The Lord is near. Have no anxiety at all, but in everything, by prayer and petition, with thanksgiving, make your requests known to God. Then the peace of God that surpasses all understanding will guard your hearts and minds in Christ Jesus. (Philippians 4:4–7)*

The Operative Question

This is the path of life that God has called us to. And to follow this path is what we long for. We now know that loving God with our heart, soul, mind, and strength means engaging all the powers of our human nature in the great adventure of seeking first the kingdom of God. But what does it look like to actually do that? How do we go from our immature state of loving to a mature state of loving? We love God already with our heart, soul, mind, and strength—otherwise we wouldn't have read this far. But what activities can we engage in to continue feeding the growth in virtue that will lead us to full maturity, to loving God with *all our all*? That is what the remainder of this book will look into.

S

Questions for Personal Reflection or Group Discussion

1. What idea in this chapter struck you most and why?

2. When you think of "holiness" and "virtue," what's the first thing that comes to mind? Does that accurately reflect the vitality and abundance that those terms are meant to evoke?

3. How would you define "happiness"? How does that definition compare with the vision of fulfillment we get from God's revelation in Jesus?

4. Frustration is always the result of unmet expectations. The more our expectations are in harmony with the truth, the less we will experience frustration. One truth that today's world—so focused on consumerism—wants us to forget is that we can never have perfect happiness until we get to heaven. But when we forget that truth, we will begin to expect perfect happiness on earth. That's a false expectation that fills us with a constant underlying frustration. What will you do today to remind yourself that you are only a pilgrim in this world?

    - I will unite some small suffering to Christ's suffering on the cross through a prayer of self-offering.

- I will try to laugh instead of to cry over spilled milk (i.e., the little, frustrating foibles of daily life).
- (Write your own resolution) I will____________________________.

Concluding Prayer

Oh! how I love you, Jesus! My soul aspires to you
And yet for one day only my simple prayer I pray!
Come reign within my heart, smile tenderly on me,
Today, dear Lord, today.

But if I dare take thought of what the morrow brings,
That fills my fickle heart with dreary, dull dismay;
I crave, indeed, my God, trials and sufferings,
But only for today!

O sweetest Star of heaven! O Virgin, spotless, blest,
Shining with Jesus' light, guiding to Him my way!
O Mother! 'neath your veil let my tired spirit rest,
For this brief passing day!

Soon shall I fly afar among the holy choirs,
Then shall be mine the joy that never knows decay;
And then my lips shall sing, to heaven's angelic lyres,
The eternal, glad Today!

—St. Thérèse of Lisieux[24]

24 http://www.catholicspiritualdirection.org/poemstherese.pdf

Chapter 25
A Profile of Virtue

[St. Paul] is concerned with the morally good or bad works, or better the permanent dispositions—virtues and vices—which are the fruit of submission to or of resistance to the saving action of the Holy Spirit. Consequently the Apostle writes: "If we live by the Spirit, let us also walk by the Spirit" (Galatians 5:25).

—St. John Paul II, *Dominum et Vivificantem,* 55

AS HUMAN BEINGS in the world of time and space, we have to interact constantly with three basic realities: 1) things that cause or promise to cause pleasure; 2) things that cause or threaten to cause pain or harm; and 3) other persons. Our passions tend to react automatically to pleasures and pains, as we have seen. If we form the habit of making our decisions and taking action based only on those automatic, irrational reactions, we will form vices—habits or patterns of acting that contradict what is truly good for our human nature. If we form the habit of taking into account those important emotional reactions as we make our decisions but finally taking action based on the firmer principles of faith and reason, we will form virtues. Virtues can simply be described as our natural powers acting habitually and easily in a proper manner, acting in accordance with the truth of our human nature and vocation. The more virtuous we are, the more doing-the-right-thing and experiencing the internal benefits of doing-the-right-thing—regardless of how difficult or complex that may be—become second nature.

The Cardinal Virtues

Through the ages, philosophers have identified four basic virtues that are like the hinges of our moral and spiritual life. (The word *cardinal* actually comes from the Latin word that means "hinge.") They correspond to those three realities that we interact with on a regular basis.

If we learn to govern our raw desire for pleasure in accordance with what is truly healthy and in harmony with God's purpose for our lives, we develop the cardinal virtue of *temperance*. Temperance takes different forms in relation to the different types of pleasure that we have to deal with (chastity, sobriety, meekness, humility). If we learn to govern the fear that pain and suffering inspire, so that this never impedes us from doing what is right and necessary according to God's purpose for our lives, we develop the cardinal virtue of *fortitude* or courage, whose sister virtues include patience and perseverance. If we learn to treat all other persons (God as well as our fellow human beings) with the dignity that they deserve, regardless of how we may feel about them or what they may be able to do for or against us, then we grow in the virtue of *justice*, which also has a slew of sister virtues (e.g., honesty, piety, obedience).

Those three cardinal virtues perfect the exercise of our will and emotions in relation to the types of realities that we have to interact with in this world. The fourth cardinal virtue, *prudence* or wisdom, is the development of our intelligence so that it recognizes and discerns what actions are proper (virtuous, healthy, in accordance with our true good) within the myriad and tangled situations of real life.

The Theological Virtues

When we were baptized, we were adopted into God's family, and he infused into our soul capacities to relate to him that did not belong to our pre-baptized nature. This infusion gave the life of grace to our souls. We were enabled to know God, to recognize his voice and his truth, and to accept and believe in him and in those truths that he reveals; this capacity is known as the theological virtue of *faith*. We were also given a deep impulse to expect our fulfillment in life from God himself, not from any of God's creatures, as good and beautiful as they may be. This impulse is known as the virtue, the capacity, of theological *hope*. Finally, were we given the ability, the supernatural capacity, to actually enter into interpersonal communion with the Trinity, to live in friendship with God, as if we were his equals—which by nature we are not; only through grace have we been given this potential. This capacity to engage with the Trinity in a relationship of mutual self-giving is known as the theological virtue, the soul-power, of *love*, also called divine charity.

In a sense, through the infusion of grace at baptism, God "supernaturalized" our human nature. Now faith opens and directs our intellect toward the divine light of God himself, not just to the created lights of finite truths. Now hope spurs our hearts to yearn for completeness in God himself, not only in the good things God has created. Now theological love enables us to converse with and experience an intimate, familial relationship with the infinite God, not only with fellow human beings. It's as if God altered our spiritual DNA on the day of our baptism, so that we are now *truly* members of God's family, not only legally and emotionally, in a way that no merely human adoption can make an adopted child into a member of that adopting family.

New Strength for a New Standard

This may seem abstract and impractical, but it's critical for a clear understanding of what growing in virtue really means for a Christian. Merely natural virtues, which have as their standard and measuring rod human nature unaided by grace, are no longer sufficient for the spiritual maturity we are called to. God's supernatural grace is indeed infused into our human nature, and it works from within that nature. And so the four cardinal virtues that describe the maturation of our natural powers are still valid for the Christian. But they are elevated to a new standard.

For example, self-preservation of the individual and the tribe was the highest value for the pagan world. This led them to see other tribes as inherently less worthy than themselves, as not deserving of the rights (justice) that members of their own tribe enjoyed. In the light of faith, however, and as members of God's family, we now know that every human person has an equal dignity based on having been created in God's image, and so all human persons have equal rights. We no longer reserve our compassion and kindness just for members of our own tribe.

To take another example, we can reflect on how our supernatural faith and hope in God enables Christians to put earthly comfort and success in second place, behind their top priority of friendship with Jesus Christ. This is how so many Christian martyrs have found the strength to refuse to renounce that friendship even in the face of seductive blandishments and agonizing tortures. Only because of this supernatural DNA, this infused grace of God at work within us, does anything in the gospel make sense to us and attract us. Only faith, hope, and love, for example, could motivate a Christian to renounce the goods of this world completely and follow a vocation to the monastery or the cloister: "What profit is there for one to gain the whole world and forfeit his life?" (Mark 8:36).

S

Questions for Personal Reflection or Group Discussion

1. What idea in this chapter struck you most and why?

2. How would you explain the concept of Christian virtue to someone who asked you about it?

3. Up to this point in your life, what have you consciously and consistently done to exercise the virtues of faith, hope, and charity?

4. When dealing with definitions, as we did in this chapter, virtue can seem dry and abstract. But in fact it's intensely practical, and it's relevant to everything we experience on a daily basis. When we're stuck in traffic and our blood starts to boil, the virtue of patience (a sister virtue of fortitude) keeps us calm and collected instead of getting exhausted by mild (or not so mild) road rage. When the pleasures of video games or TV or social media threaten to sabotage our sense of responsibility to God, family, and ourselves, the virtue of temperance enables us to click the off button. When we are treated unfairly at work or we get laid off and we see no solution on the horizon, the virtue of hope enables us

to continue forward without imploding—we know that resurrections come after crucifixions. What will you do today to exercise intentionally one of the theological virtues?

- I will go out of my way to do something kind for someone I don't really get along with on a natural level, without looking for anything in return (love).
- I will buy a crucifix to hang on my bedroom wall and have a priest bless it (faith).
- I will stop putting something off simply because I am afraid of failing—I will take the next step out of confidence in God (hope).
- (Write your own resolution) I will______________________________.

Concluding Prayer

Lord, holy Father, almighty and ever-living God, I thank you.
For though I am a sinner and your unprofitable servant, you have fed me with the precious Body and Blood of your Son, our Lord Jesus Christ. You did this not because I deserved it, but because you are kind and merciful.
I pray that this holy Communion may not add to my guilt and punishment, but may lead me to forgiveness and salvation.
May it be for me the armor of faith and a shield of good will.
May it remove my vices and extinguish my evil tendencies.
May it bring me charity and patience, humility and obedience, and may it strengthen my power to do every kind of good.
May it be a firm defense against the deceit of all my enemies, visible and invisible.
May it perfectly satisfy all my yearnings, bodily and spiritual.
May it unite me more closely to you, the one true God.
May it bring me to the happy possession of the goal I am seeking.

—Prayer after Communion, St. Thomas Aquinas[25]

25 Roman Missal, Appendix of Prayers after Communion.

Chapter 26
Exercising the Virtues

It is not a question of simply knowing what God wants from each of us in the various situations of life. The individual must do what God wants, as we are reminded in the words that Mary, the Mother of Jesus, addressed to the servants at Cana: "Do whatever he tells you" (John 2:5).
—St. John Paul II, *Christifideles Laici*, 58

THE PATH OF growing in Christian virtue, of developing all the powers of our nature in harmony with their true purposes, is the path that will lead us to the fulfillment that we are created for and that we long for. But how do we grow in virtue?

Growth in virtue requires exercising virtue. It sounds so simple. And it is. Human nature is made this way. When we nourish and use the powers of our soul properly, they grow, just like muscles. If a young man wants to improve his tennis game, he needs to keep playing tennis; he needs to exercise his skills and abilities so they develop. Just thinking and dreaming about it will get him nowhere. Likewise, if we want to mature in our love for God, if we want to grow in the virtues that unite our heart, mind, emotions, and will to the Lord so we can have deeper communion with him, then we need to nourish and exercise them. And only in that communion will we find lasting happiness.

The Virtues Grow Together

The history of Christian spirituality has provided various categorizations of the different virtues. It can be helpful to study these and delve, for example, into the distinctions between courage and perseverance, or chastity and purity, or distributive justice and commutative justice. Yet, since the human person is an organic whole, when an individual exercises one virtue, his or her entire spiritual organism is engaged and therefore benefits. In a sense, it is impossible to grow in one of the fundamental virtues without also growing in the others. Just as a baby's five fingers all grow out together—the middle finger doesn't grow to maturity first before the pinky starts to grow—so the Christian who responds docilely and generously to the guidance of the Holy Spirit grows in all the basic virtues simultaneously. The other side of this coin is also true: If we are negligently deficient in any one of the basic virtues, we will only have limited progress in the others. It's important to keep this in mind when we begin discussing what activities you can engage in to exercise your virtue.

The Primary Spiritual Workout

One activity exercises every Christian virtue simultaneously and intensely. Without it, spiritual maturity is impossible. This activity is prayer.

Prayer is conversation with God, listening to him and speaking to him. It exercises faith, because God's presence, his voice, is almost always mediated by something—the Bible, the beauty of nature, music, other spiritual books. Talking with God simply can't happen without faith: "For we walk by faith, not by sight" (2 Corinthians 5:7, RSV).

Prayer exercises hope, because we don't always feel immediate consolation and satisfaction in prayer; our confidence in God's faithfulness motivates us to continue investing in prayer even when results seem long in coming. We know that by praying we are following Christ's command to "store up treasures in heaven, where neither moth nor decay destroys, nor thieves break in and steal" (Matthew 6:20), but often we don't actually enjoy those treasures during our time of prayer.

Christian prayer exercises charity, because we address God as our Father, and we open our hearts to him just as he opens his heart to us; Christian prayer is much more than a mere self-tranquilizing technique or formulaic superstition. The Catechism reminds us of this powerfully when it summarizes how we must engage with the mystery of God's revelation in Christ:

> *This mystery, then, requires that the faithful believe in it, that they celebrate it, and that they live from it in a vital and personal relationship with the living and true God. This relationship is prayer.* (*CCC*, 2558)

Prayer exercises the cardinal virtues, too, because God deserves our worship and confidence (justice), because prayer takes effort and self-sacrifice since it is not always pleasing (temperance and fortitude), because praying involves overcoming fears and doubts about whether God loves us or what others may say about us (fortitude), and because the true value of prayer is evident only to the wise (prudence). Prayer truly is the one activity that will most help us exercise our heart, mind, soul, and strength in loving God.

How Much Should I Pray?

In our post-modern, secularized culture, growth in prayer requires commitment and discipline—remember, we are to love God with *all* our mind and strength, not only when we happen to feel like it. The basic staples that Christians should include in their spiritual diet include daily, weekly, and seasonal commitments. These will change, vary, and develop as our relationship with God deepens, but here is a sensible starting guideline.

On a daily basis, we need to engage in both vocal and mental prayer. Vocal prayer uses prayers composed by other people—like the prayers that have appeared at the end of each chapter in this book. We can find favorite vocal prayers and use them to offer our day to God in the morning, to put the day in his hands in the evening, or to check in with him at noontime. Mental prayer is more intimate. It involves listening to God through reflecting on a Bible passage or a spiritual commentary on the Bible or on some aspect of our faith. That reflection spurs us to speak to God in the silence of our hearts, using our own words—thanking him, asking for forgiveness, praising him, or simply opening our hearts to him. Without daily mental prayer, without a daily God-time, our other efforts to grow spiritually lose their grip; we end up just spinning our wheels. Ten minutes a day of mental prayer, preferably in the morning, is a reasonable place to start. Many solid and substantial daily devotionals are available to help our mental prayer.

Weekly, God commands us to come alongside the rest of our spiritual family to worship him by attending Sunday Mass (and living the Lord's Day well). We should do everything possible to receive Holy Communion on the Lord's Day. The Eucharist is the grace-filled food for our Christian journey, without which we will surely "collapse on the way" (Matthew 15:32).

Seasonally, we should follow closely the rhythms of the liturgical year, using the sacrament of confession (another guaranteed outpouring of grace) during each period and staying engaged in the parish celebrations (processions, penitential services, special feast days). The Holy Spirit uses this liturgical rhythm to form our hearts according to God's priorities and not the world's. A yearly spiritual retreat or pilgrimage is also as essential as a yearly medical checkup, if we are serious about seeking first Christ's kingdom.

Books and seminars and formation videos that can teach us how to live more and more deeply each of these prayer commitments abound (you can find some recommendations in the Appendix). But none of them can make the commitment for us, and none of them can pray for us. Not even God can do that. We must decide to put our heart, soul, mind, and strength to work in "seeking the face of the Lord" through the great gift of Christian prayer (see Psalm 27:8).

S

Questions for Personal Reflection or Group Discussion

1. What idea in this chapter struck you most and why?

2. How would you describe the frequency and quality of your prayer life?

3. When have you had a positive experience of prayer? What led to it, and what did you do to follow up with it?

4. Archbishop Fulton Sheen created a television program called *Life Is Worth Living* that became the highest-rated prime-time show in Ameri-

can during the fifties. He reached tens of millions of viewers every single week. When asked what his "secret" was, he said that it all flowed from his unbreakable commitment to spend at least a full hour in personal prayer, in a chapel where the Holy Eucharist was present, every single morning. What will you do today to begin improving your prayer life?

- I will buy a good Catholic prayer book.
- I will talk to someone I know who has a mature prayer life and ask them how they got there.
- I will find a friend and make a daily prayer pact, agreeing to hold each other accountable for this commitment.
- (Write your own resolution) I will______________________________.

Concluding Prayer

My Jesus, on this new day I renew my consecration and offer myself to you, for you to make use of my soul, my body, my strength, my mind, and my will as you please. I am totally yours; keep me faithful to your friendship. Enable me to live this day with the eager desire to glorify the Father, fulfilling his will faithfully and constantly. Give me a steadfast heart, that will not forsake you by squandering my love, a generous chaste heart, unstained by any unworthy affection, an unselfish heart, only consumed by your love and the interests of your kingdom, a conquering heart, like your very own. Grant, Lord Jesus, that all of us who are consecrated to you in your holy Catholic Church will be more faithful and courageous apostles of your kingdom. Amen.

—from the Prayer Book of the Legionaries of Christ

Chapter 27
Spiritual Input

Since man can neither live nor understand himself without love, I want to appeal to you to grow in humanity, to give absolute priority to the values of the spirit, and to transform yourselves into "new men" *by increasingly recognizing and accepting the presence of God in your life: the presence of a God who is Love; of a Father who loves each one of us for the whole of eternity, who created us by love and who loved us so much that he gave up his Only Son to forgive us our sins, to reconcile us to Him, and to enable us to live with Him in a communion of love which will never end.*

—St. John Paul II, Message for World Youth Day, 1987

IN OUR POST-CHRISTIAN culture, the spiritual, moral, and intellectual atmosphere that surrounds our daily activities contains anti-Christian values. Our cultural environment is polluted by a worldview that promotes hedonism, secularism, relativism, consumerism, and a host of other toxic perspectives. These can steadily corrode our Christ-centered way of seeing ourselves, others, and the world around us, just as coal dust gradually sickens a miner's respiratory system.

In previous eras, popular culture itself was imbued with the Christian worldview, so even popular books and dramas reinforced the Christian value system. But now that is no longer the case. Instead, our minds are flooded every day by messages (advertisements, films, TV shows, news, music) that directly contradict the Christian worldview. That will have its effect on how we think and what we value. In fact, this is one of the reasons the Church is suffering so much from so-called cafeteria Catholicism.

Cafeteria Catholics get much of their Catholic formation from secular sources (*The New York Times, Newsweek*), and so they simply can't understand why the Church would ever suggest alternatives to such popular and seemingly reasonable (from a secular point of view) propositions like artificial contraception, artificial reproduction, and gay marriage.

Because of this ongoing flood of secular ideas, we have to consciously nourish our minds with authentic Christian teaching in order to avoid being poisoned. If we don't intentionally and intelligently counteract this cultural pollution, we will fall away from healthy spiritual fervor into spiritual mediocrity, which is only a short distance away from habitual, soul-killing rebellion against and abandonment of the one thing needed for our authentic fulfillment now and forever (see Luke 10:42). We have to breathe fresh spiritual air every day if we want to keep our spiritual organism healthy and growing.

Spiritual Reading

Spiritual reading is one tried and true antidote to cultural pollution. It consists of regularly (daily is best) reading something that explains an aspect of Catholic truth in an attractive, enriching way. Its function is to help reinforce and deepen our Christian view of ourselves and of the world around us. It's ongoing formation for a Christian mind.

Spiritual reading is either instructive or refreshing. It either informs our minds so that we learn to think and understand more and more in harmony with God's revelation, or it refreshes what we already know or have learned by making it shine out more clearly once again. In either case, it counteracts the seductive, secularizing messages that saturate our cultural milieu. This is why it's such an important spiritual discipline. It plants seeds of Christian truth in our mind, and they grow and germinate in our subconscious as we go about our daily business. These seeds often flower during our times of mental prayer. In fact, spiritual reading frequently provides topics, ideas, or insights that are excellent material for Christian meditation.

How to Do Spiritual Reading

Spiritual reading differs from regular reading not only in the content, but also in the method. You don't need to spend a lot of time doing spiritual reading, and you don't need to read fast. The idea is simply to taste, chew on, and swallow some healthy Catholic concepts every single day.

The distinction between spiritual reading and mental prayer (or meditation) is the end result. The goal of your meditation is to converse with the Lord about what matters to him and what matters to you. The reflection and consideration that forms part of your meditation is meant to spur that conversation in your heart. The goal of spiritual reading is to inform your mind; it doesn't advance or finish with a prayerful conversation (though that can sometimes pop up spontaneously, which is fine).

Today's Catholics have at their fingertips an abundance of good material for spiritual reading—old and new books easy to find, old and new articles and websites easy to access. But if you're not a reader, or if you think you don't have time, you can get creative. Listening to recordings of spiritual talks, homilies, or conferences (or books on tape, or even good Catholic podcasts) while you drive or exercise can also do the trick.

An Eye to Entertainment

We all need to rest and relax sometimes, and enjoying a good movie, game, novel, show, or trip downtown can often help that happen. Unfortunately, however, this area of human endeavor has also been affected by post-Christian cultural pollution. Pastimes we engage in for necessary rest and relaxation should be both enjoyable and edifying. They should refresh us, but they should also encourage our Christian values—or at least not discourage them.

This doesn't mean that we should hide away in a Christian bunker somewhere and avoid looking at or listening to anything not explicitly biblical—the Puritan experiment failed in the end, after all, and generations of saints have nourished their minds and hearts on all the great artistic achievements of the human family, including pagan ones. But it does mean that we need to be smart and intentional about the food we give our imagination and the stimulation we give our emotions. We need to avoid input that could be an occasion of sin for us or for others, and we need to find out what truly helps us get the rest and relaxation necessary to maintain a healthy emotional and physiological profile. Proper rest and entertainment are in the service of our life mission; they are not our goal. Christians don't live for the weekend; we live for loving Christ and building up his kingdom.

News and Current Events

A final area of input that can help us show and grow our love for God has to do with staying informed about current issues and events. With the digital news cycle that never ends, we can be tempted to think that we need to know the backstory behind every headline that pops onto our mental screen, from whatever source. Not true. The digital world of information allows us, for the first time in history, to stay duly informed about the issues and events most relevant to us as Christians. We can choose the sources of our information so that we fill our minds with what we choose to think about, not what a secular producer wants us to think about. And that choice should be made regularly and intentionally with our life's true purpose in mind.

In short, moving forward along the path of Christian virtue requires paying attention to the map the Lord has given us and avoiding seductive sidetracks. As St. Paul put it:

> *Finally, brothers, whatever is true, whatever is honorable, whatever is just, whatever is pure, whatever is lovely, whatever is gracious, if there is any excellence and if there is anything worthy of praise, think about these things.* (Philippians 4:8, RSV)

S

Questions for Personal Reflection or Group Discussion

1. What idea in this chapter struck you most and why?

2. In your daily life, what are the most common sources of the ideas that go into your mind and imagination?

3. What do you usually do for rest and relaxation? What can you do to make your relaxation activities healthier?

4. One of the most admirable and inspiring aspects of monastic architecture is the balance it achieves between visual silence and visual stimulus. In order to create an atmosphere conducive to prayer, recollection, and interior depth, architects carefully choose and arrange all the external décor, from the plants in the courtyard to the paintings on the walls of the dining room. The result is a physical atmosphere of harmony, beauty, and a sense of peace that you can almost touch. This is one reason monasteries have been able to produce so many saints. What will you do today to fill your mind and soul with what is true, honorable, just, pure, lovely, and gracious?

    - I will visit a monastery and spend some time absorbing the atmosphere.
    - I will decide at the start of each week what I will use for entertainment and recreation, and then I will stick to that decision.
    - I will consciously decide how much time each day (or week) I really need to dedicate to staying caught up on current events, and then I will stick to that time allotment.
    - (Write your own resolution) I will______________________________.

Concluding Prayer

Lord Jesus,
I give you my hands to do your work.
I give you my feet to follow your path.
I give you my eyes to see as you see.
I give you my tongue to speak your words.
I give you my mind so you can think in me.
I give you my spirit so you can pray in me.
Above all I give you my heart so in me you can love your Father and all people.
I give you my whole self so you can grow in me, till it is you who live and work and pray in me. Amen.

—from the Prayer Book of the Regnum Christi Movement

Chapter 28
Spiritual Allies

To be able to discover the actual will of the Lord in our lives always involves the following: a receptive listening to the Word of God and the Church, fervent and constant prayer, recourse to a wise and loving spiritual guide, and a faithful discernment of the gifts and talents given by God, as well as the diverse social and historic situations in which one lives.
—St. John Paul II, *Christifideles Laici*, 58

ALTHOUGH EACH ONE of us has a personal relationship with God, that relationship takes root and grows within a larger network of relationships within the Church. When we are baptized, we are inserted into Christ's mystical body; we are made members of "a chosen race, a royal priesthood, a holy nation, a people of his own," as St. Peter reminds us (1 Peter 2:9).

The Christian Identification Card

The fact that we are called to be Christ's companions (in the plural), called to walk with him in loving fellowship with our brothers and sisters in the Church, is so important to Jesus that he made it the main identification badge of all Christians. During the Last Supper, he told his apostles that to be his disciples meant following his commandments, and he condensed those commandments to one: "Love one another as I have loved you" (John 15:12).

He went on to say that the world will recognize us as his followers precisely through our fellowship, through our living in love and faith-filled union with each other: "This is how all will know that you are my disciples, if you have love for one another" (John 13:35). The key theological reason behind the importance Jesus gives to this loving unity among his followers goes back to the very beginning when God created us. He created the human family "in his image...in the image of God he created them" (Genesis 1:27). God's core identity is a Trinity: one divine nature and three divine persons. He is a community, a family—a unique one, because he is only one God, not three gods. The Church is God's way of redeeming this damaged aspect of the fallen human race, this divine image in which we were created:

> *[God] calls together all men, scattered and divided by sin, into the unity of his family, the Church. To accomplish this, when the fullness of time had come, God sent his Son as the Redeemer and Savior.* (*CCC*, 1)

But there is a practical reason, too. Simply put, we need each other. We can't finish our Christian pilgrimage alone. We need the strength, the light, the guidance, the encouragement, and the help that comes from traveling with other pilgrims.

The First Form of Fellowship

The first and fundamental manifestation of Christian fellowship comes in the worship of the Christian community, and this is expressed most intensely and fully in the celebration of the sacraments. Christian fellowship is only Christian because its core is Christ himself. This is why Jesus summoned his first apostles "that they might be with him" (Mark 3:14). He is the Savior; he is the Redeemer. It was through the mystery of his passion, death, and resurrection that the Church—the renewed communion of mankind with God and in God with each other—was born.

The celebration of the sacraments links the Church to that mystery. The whole liturgical life of the new people of God is like the heartbeat of that Church: "Through the liturgy, Christ, our redeemer and high priest, continues the work of our redemption in, with, and through his Church"

(*CCC*, 1069). The liturgy also introduces us to the spiritually fruitful, and even necessary, devotion to saints and angels and, in a special way, to the Blessed Virgin Mary—important allies in our spiritual battles.

The Sunday Eucharist is the center of the Church's liturgical life. But the other sacraments are also opportunities to live and grow and benefit from this fellowship. We go to confession to ask for and receive God's forgiveness and also for reconciliation with the community that we damage by our sins. We comfort the sick and dying by bringing them Christ's holy anointing. We gather with our fellow Christian pilgrims for baptisms and confirmations, for marriages and ordinations, supporting and being supported by one another even as we open up the floodgates of God's grace toward every corner of human experience.

And the primary place for this sacramental fellowship is the parish—a kind of local incarnation, through the Church's diocesan structure, of the universal Church. Staying plugged in and contributing to our parishes or our religious communities is the bread and butter of Christian fellowship.

The Second Form of Fellowship

The Christian family, built up around the sacrament of marriage, is another place where this loving fellowship is meant to be lived out. In fact, Christian tradition, spiritualizing a term used originally used to refer only to buildings, has come to see the family as a "domestic church." The natural bonds and affection that flow from familial relations are bridges, so to speak, over which God's grace can flow in wonderful abundance if we consciously build our families around their real center: Jesus and his truth, his love, his mission.

It has never been easy to do this, because the effects of original sin are still with us, and our selfishness and woundedness make healthy family life a demanding work in progress. In a post-Christian culture, where family life is under attack legally, economically, educationally, and culturally, building the domestic church is harder than ever; it takes an almost heroic effort. But God's grace will always come to our aid.

The Role of Faith-Based Friendships

Friendship is one of the most beautiful human experiences, and Jesus himself praised and prized it. "I no longer call you slaves," he told his apostles at the Last Supper, "because a slave does not know what his master is doing. I have called you friends, because I have told you everything I have heard from my Father" (John 15:15). Friendship has been valued in every period and place of human history, even long before the time of Christ. It is another manifestation of our being created in the image of God, created to live in communion of life with other persons. It contributes joy, comfort, inspiration, and meaning to our lives.

But with the coming of Christ, even this beautiful human reality has been enhanced. A faith-based, Christ-centered friendship is a deeper, stronger, and longer-lasting friendship than any of the ancient philosophers could have imagined, for one simple reason: Christ himself is part of it. He promised this in one of the most beautiful verses of the New Testament: "For where two or three are gathered together in my name, there am I in the midst of them" (Matthew 18:20, RSV).

Faith-based friendships are an important aspect of Christian fellowship; they help keep us accountable, they help support us in times of temptation, they help heal our emotional wounds, they spur us on to growth in virtue, they delight and comfort us at the deeper levels of our soul, and they help keep Jesus close to us.

Of course, this doesn't mean that we can't have non-Christian friends, but we do need to make a point of investing in some friendships that are built with natural as well as supernatural ties. If our faith is our highest priority, we will feel the need for friends who share that priority. And if we don't look for them and invest in them, we may gradually find our priorities getting confused. St. Paul gave a warning in this regard to the Christians in Corinth: "Do not be led astray," he wrote to them; "bad company corrupts good morals" (1 Corinthians 15:33, RSV).

The Benefits of Spiritual Direction

Finally, growing to spiritual maturity requires the direct assistance of a spiritual coach, which Christian tradition generally calls a spiritual director. We need an ongoing relationship with someone who knows the spiritual ropes, who has traveled the road ahead of us and has a healthy share of the gift of counsel, who can help uncover our blind spots and discern how the Holy Spirit is moving in our lives and how we should respond. We need teachers, mentors, coaches, trainers, and guides in every other area of human life where we want to improve and grow, so it only makes sense that we would need one here as well. As Pope Benedict XVI explained to a group of future spiritual directors:

> *As she has never failed to do, again today the Church continues to recommend the practice of spiritual direction, not only to all those who wish to follow the Lord up close, but to every Christian who wishes to live responsibly his baptism, that is, the new life in Christ.*[26]

S

Questions for Personal Reflection or Group Discussion

1. What idea in this chapter struck you most and why?

2. What characteristics of your daily life make it hard for you to have meaningful fellowship?

3. What have been your most meaningful family experiences? What can you do to contribute more to building up your family as a domestic church?

4. The Book of Proverbs observes: "Iron is sharpened by iron; one person sharpens another" (Proverbs 27:17). What will you do today to take better advantage of this part of your Christian life?

    - I will invest meaningfully in one of my faith-based friendships by spending time with someone I haven't spent much time with lately.
    - I will start asking around to see about finding a spiritual director.
    - I will take some time to see all of the different programs and activities offered by my parish, and I will sign up for one of them.
    - (Write your own resolution) I will____________________________.

26 Benedict XVI, Address, May 19, 2011.

Concluding Prayer

It is truly right and just that we should always give you thanks, Lord holy Father, almighty and eternal God.
For you do not cease to spur us on to possess a more abundant life and, being rich in mercy, you constantly offer pardon and call on sinners to trust in your forgiveness alone.
Never did you turn away from us, and, though time and again we have broken your covenant, you have bound the human family to yourself through Jesus your Son, our Redeemer, with a new bond of love so tight that it can never be undone.
Even now you set before your people a time of grace and reconciliation, and, as they turn back to you in spirit, you grant them hope in Christ Jesus and a desire to be of service to all, while they entrust themselves more fully to the Holy Spirit.
And so, filled with wonder, we extol the power of your love, and proclaiming our joy at the salvation that comes from you, we join in the heavenly hymn of countless hosts, as without end we acclaim…

—Roman Missal, Preface for Reconciliation I

Chapter 29
Hungering for God's Will

Yes, discovering Christ is the finest adventure of your life. But it is not enough to discover Him just once. Discovering Him becomes an ongoing invitation to seek Him always more, to come to know Him still better through prayer, participating in the sacraments, meditating on his Word, through catechesis and listening to the teachings of the Church. This is our most important task, as St. Paul had well understood when he wrote: "For me, indeed, to live is Christ" (Philippians 1:21).
—St. John Paul II, Message for World Youth Day, August 1989

JESUS IS THE center of every authentically Christian life. Loving God with all our heart, soul, mind, and strength means loving Jesus more and more and more, because Jesus is God-become-man, God-with-us. And loving Jesus means following him, learning from him, obeying him, becoming more like him, and letting him be our strength and salvation, as he continually invites us to do:

> *Come to me, all you who labor and are burdened, and I will give you rest. Take my yoke upon you and learn from me, for I am meek and humble of heart; and you will find rest for your selves. For my yoke is easy, and my burden light. (Matthew 11:28–30)*

What Made Jesus Tick?

If the spiritual life is, in its most basic elements, nothing less than following Christ and imitating him—and that is precisely how St. Paul summed it up: "Be imitators of me, as I am of Christ" (1 Corinthians 11:1)—then Christ's deepest desire should be our deepest desire. During his life on earth, his very food, the thing that he hungered for and the thing that nourished and strengthened him, was "to do the will of the one who sent me" (John 4:34). So central was this idea to his life and teaching that he placed it at the very heart of the one prayer that he taught us, the Our Father: "This is how you are to pray: Our Father in heaven, hallowed be your name, your kingdom come, *your will be done,* on earth as in heaven…" (Matthew 6:9–10, emphasis added).

What Is God's Will?

The Father's will—finding it, accepting it, and carrying it out with love—was the rule for Christ's life, and so it should be the rule for the life of every Christian. And indeed, if we make this our food, as Jesus did, then our heart, soul, mind, and strength will find themselves fully engaged in our task of loving God, because the essence of love is union, becoming one with the beloved.

God's will is his wise and loving project for the full flourishing of all his creatures, especially those of us created in his own image and likeness. By striving to identify with that project in the here and now of our daily lives, we become co-workers in bringing it to completion. What greater love could we show him than that? And what more direct way could we find to achieve the purpose for which we were created? This is why Jesus, who modeled perfectly the love and purpose we are called to pursue, hungered and yearned "to do the will of the one who sent me" (John 4:34). As he explained to his persecutors: "I cannot do anything on my own…. I do not seek my own will but the will of the one who sent me" (John 5:30).

But the phrase *God's will* can be abused. People have distorted it to justify irresponsible passivity in the face of evil, self-centered and damaging manipulation of others, and exaggerated asceticism. We need to unpack the term so we can better understand what Jesus wants and better unite ourselves to him. Breaking down the concept into two broad sub-categories will help avoid confusion. From our human perspective, God's will can be either *indicative* or *permissive*.

God's Indicative Will

God can indicate that he wants us to do certain things. This is his indicative will (as opposed to his permissive will, the things he permits to happen without actually commanding them; this will be discussed in the next chapter). God's indicative will always flows from his wisdom and his love. In other words, whatever he wants us to do is for our greatest good. In this category we find the Ten Commandments, the commandments of the New Testament, the commandments and teachings of the Church, the responsibilities of our state in life, and specific inspirations of the Holy Spirit. If we want to know God's will for our lives, those are the places we need to start.

The field of God's indicative will is vast. It touches all the normal activities and relationships of every day, which are the arenas where, through our choices, we grow in virtue or in vice, thus deepening or dampening our communion with God. It also includes the endless possibilities of the works of mercy (feeding the hungry, instructing the ignorant, comforting the sorrowful, etc.), by which we carry out our Lord's commandment to "love your neighbor as yourself" (Mark 12:31).

Going Even Deeper

Yet God's indicative will not only consists of *what* we do, but also in *how* we do it. This opens up another path of growth in Christian virtue, most especially the theological virtues. We can wash the dishes (responsibilities of our state in life) with resentment and self-pity, or with love, care, and supernatural joy. We can attend Sunday Mass (the third commandment and a commandment of the Church) apathetically and reluctantly, or with conviction, faith, and attention. We can drive to work (responsibilities of our state in life) seething at the traffic jams, or exercising patience. When we ask ourselves, "What is God's will for me?"

88 percent of the time (more or less), God's indicative will is crystal clear: lovingly follow the commandments, lovingly carry out our daily responsibilities, and look for practical ways to love our neighbors as God has loved us. To seek, accept, embrace, and fulfill this will for our lives is

the surest way to engaging our heart, soul, mind, and strength fully in loving God.

Much of the Church's tradition of spiritual teaching is dedicated to exploring the implications of and the reasons behind these indicative commandments; the more thoroughly we understand them, the more of our heart, soul, mind, and strength we can put into obeying them. And that obedience is the path to the wisdom, peace, and fulfillment we yearn for—what Jesus referred to as blessedness: "Blessed are those who hear the word of God and observe it" (Luke 11:28).

S

Questions for Personal Reflection or Group Discussion

1. What idea in this chapter struck you most and why?

2. Make a list of the responsibilities of your state in life and put them in order of importance. How easily and fully do you recognize and embrace God's will in those responsibilities?

3. How deeply do you hunger to discover and fulfill God's will in your life?

4. Although most of the time we know what God's indicative will is for us (through the commandments, Christ's teachings, and our normal life responsibilities), there are times when we aren't sure: *Should I accept this new job offer? Should we move? Should I join the seminary? Should I intervene in a family member's difficult situation?* In these cases, the traditional path of discerning God's will for us -consists in asking for light and guidance in prayer, getting good advice from trusted sources, and taking time to reflect on the different options. Usually in the end the path becomes clear. And even if it doesn't, as long as we have done our homework, so to speak, God will work with whatever we decide. What will you do today to become more aware of God's will for your life?

    - I will ask myself after each meal, "God, what is your will for me right now?" And I'll listen for whatever answer comes to my mind and my heart.

- I will find and read a good article describing one of my key life areas (a good article on fatherhood or motherhood, for example, or one on ethics in the workplace, etc.).
- I will pay attention to my initial reaction the next time I am not sure what to do. How spontaneously do I involve God in my efforts to find an answer?
- (Write your own resolution) I will____________________________.

Concluding Prayer

Holy Spirit, gentle guest and consoler of my soul,
Enlighten my mind to know the divine will for me;
Inflame my heart to love it passionately;
Strengthen my will to accomplish it as perfectly as you ask of me;
Lastly, Spirit of love, grant me the grace I need to respond faithfully to your holy inspirations. Amen.

—from the Prayer Book of the Legionaries of Christ

Chapter 30
Taking Up the Cross

For if, in fact, the Cross was to human eyes Christ's emptying of himself, at the same time it was in the eyes of God his being lifted up. On the Cross, Christ attained and fully accomplished his mission: by fulfilling the will of the Father, he at the same time fully realized himself.... Suffering is also an invitation to manifest the moral greatness of man, his spiritual maturity. Proof of this has been given, down through the generations, by the martyrs and confessors of Christ, faithful to the words; "And do not fear those who kill the body, but cannot kill the soul" (Matthew 10:28).

—St. John Paul II, *Salvifici Doloris*, 22

SEEKING AND FULFILLING God's indicative will in our lives—his commandments, his inspirations, and the normal responsibilities that we have simply because we are members of a family, a workplace, a community, and a society—is our sure path to spiritual growth. It unites us to Christ, who made his Father's will the overarching rule of his life, and thereby deepens more and more our intimate union and communion with God. And that is the source of our happiness.

God's Permissive Will

But the phrase *God's will* also touches another category of life-experience: suffering. Suffering, of one type or another, is our constant companion as we journey through this fallen world. God has revealed that suffering was not part of his original plan, but rather the offspring of original sin, which shattered the harmony of God's creation. His indicative will to our first parents in the Garden of Eden was for them not to "eat the fruit of "the tree of the knowledge of good and evil" (Genesis 2:17, RSV). They disobeyed. Human nature fell; creation fell; evil attained a certain predominance in the human condition, giving rise to "the overwhelming misery which oppresses men and their inclination towards evil and death" (*CCC*, 403).

Here is where the distinction between God's indicative and permissive will comes in. God did not desire or command Adam and Eve to rebel against his plan, but he did *permit* them to do so; he gave them a certain degree of freedom that made disobedience to his indicative will (moral evil) possible. Likewise, throughout human history, God does not will evil to happen, but he does *permit* it. He certainly didn't explicitly will the Holocaust, for example, but, on the other hand, he certainly did permit it. His indicative will doesn't lead to the abuse of innocent children, but his permissive will sometimes allows his free creatures to disobey his indicative will and commit such evils.

The question of why God permits some evil and the suffering that comes from it, even the suffering of innocents, is an extremely hard question to answer. Only the Christian faith as a whole gives a satisfactory response to it, a response that can gradually penetrate our hearts and minds through prayer, study, and the help of God's grace.

St. Augustine's short answer is worth mentioning, however. He wrote that if God permits evil, it is only because he knows he can bring out of that evil a greater good. We may not see that greater good right away; we may not see it at all during our earthly journey, in fact. But Christ's resurrection (Easter Sunday) is the unbreakable and undying promise that God's omnipotence and wisdom are never trumped by the apparent triumphs of evil and suffering (Good Friday).

Thus, only by faith can we begin to understand why obedience to God's will also includes accepting the painful things that he permits, trusting that in our Christ-centered response to them (which often involves resisting and correcting evils) we will be contributing to building up his eternal kingdom in our hearts and in the world.

Take Up Your Cross

In this context we can brave a brief comment on the one condition that Jesus lays down for anyone who wants to follow him:

> *Then [Jesus] said to all, "If anyone wishes to come after me, he must deny himself and take up his cross daily and follow me. For whoever wishes to save his life will lose it, but whoever loses his life for my sake will save it."* (Luke 9:23–24)

Growing in love requires self-denial, self-forgetfulness, self-giving. And in this fallen world, self-giving is often painful (in heaven it won't be). It involves taking up the cross, just as Jesus took up his own cross in order to show the extent of his love for the Father and for us. The cross symbolizes the painful self-sacrifice that growing in love requires in this fallen world. If we truly desire to grow in loving God, to learn to love him with all our all, we will have to carry crosses.

The cross is suffering made fruitful through faith and love. When God's indicative or permissive will in our life contradicts our natural preference (our self-centered, human will), we experience the cross. His will is like the vertical beam, and our natural preference is like the horizontal beam. When they are opposed, we are faced with a grace-filled opportunity. By choosing to accept God's will when we would prefer something else, we exercise our faith, hope, and love more intensely than in any other possible situation. We show that we trust him, not because he fits into our limited, human calculations, but precisely because we believe and hope in his infinite wisdom, power, and goodness. *That's* the supernatural virtue that unites us more fully to God, deepening our trust in him, the trust which is found at the heart of all interpersonal relationships. And when we exercise that virtue more intensely, it grows more quickly and surely, and our communion with God expands and deepens.

The High Road to Holiness

The Lord sends and permits crosses in our lives because he knows they are the high road to holiness when we live them in union with him, saturating them with faith, hope, and love. As Jesus explained to his twelve apostles, almost all of whom ended up dying martyrs' deaths, he prunes the branches of his vine only so that those branches will bear more fruit:

> *I am the true vine, and my Father is the vine grower. He takes away every branch in me that does not bear fruit, and everyone that does he prunes so that it bears more fruit. (John 15:1–2)*

When we feel the pruning shears purifying our still-imperfect hearts, when we feel the weight of the cross pressing down on our limited minds and souls and strength, we know God is hard at work, and we can abandon ourselves to his care. It is then, above all, when we recognize that growth in love, holiness, and lasting happiness is only 1 percent up to us and 99 percent up to the Lord. And "therefore," as St. Paul explained, "I am content with weaknesses, insults, hardships, persecutions, and constraints, for the sake of Christ; for when I am weak, then I am strong" (2 Corinthians 12:10).

It is through bearing our crosses with Christ that we enter into the indescribable experience of joy that comes with the Resurrection. For Jesus, the darkness and suffering of Good Friday blossomed into the brilliant light of Easter Sunday—as a medieval phrase put it: *per crucem ad lucem* (through the cross to the light). If we are in him, the same will be true for us.

S

Questions for Personal Reflection or Group Discussion

1. What idea in this chapter struck you most and why?

2. How do you usually respond to suffering in your own life, and why? How do you usually respond to suffering in the lives of those around you?

3. What are your most common daily crosses right now, and how are you responding to them? How would the Lord like you to respond to them?

4. When St. Joan of Arc was being burned at the stake as a martyr, she asked for one thing. While the flames began to climb up toward her and burn her, she cried out for "a cross, hold up a cross!" One of the soldiers nearby had compassion on her and made a makeshift cross out

of pieces of wood, attaching it to the tip of his pike. He then held it up high, above the flames so St. Joan could see it. As soon as she caught sight of the cross, while the flames were burning into her own flesh, she smiled. She died gazing on Christ's cross and drawing all her strength from it. What will you do today to remind yourself that the cross is really the high road to the lasting happiness that you yearn for?

- I will watch the movie *The Passion of The Christ* from the following perspective: "Jesus suffered all of this in order to prove that absolutely nothing, not even my most horrible sins, can diminish his love for me."
- When I find myself complaining about something, I will turn that complaint into a silent prayer to God, just as Jesus did on the eve of his crucifixion when he was sweating blood in the Garden of Gethsemane.
- When some suffering is happening in my life, either to me or to a loved one, and I can't do anything to alleviate it, I will say a prayer to the Blessed Virgin Mary and use my imagination to picture her standing at the foot of the cross, helplessly watching her innocent son suffer his horrible crucifixion.
- (Write your own resolution) I will______________________________.

Concluding Prayer

Pierce, most sweet Lord Jesus, my inmost heart with the most dear and penetrating wound of your love.... May my heart ever draw near to you, seek you, glimpse you, be drawn to you and find you, think of you, speak of you, and do all that it does for the glory of your name, humbly and carefully and delightedly, eagerly and passionately and persevering to the end. Thus may you alone always be my hope, all my confidence, my joy, my rest and my peace, all that charms me, my fragrance, my sweetness, my food, my nourishment, my refuge, my help, my wisdom, my portion, my possession, my treasure. In you may my mind and my heart be fixed and secure and rooted forever without any change. Amen.

—St. Bonaventure[27]

27 Paraphrase of Prayer from St. Bonaventure, Air Maria, http://airmaria.com/category/subjects/franciscan-things/page/2/.

Conclusion

RESPONDING TO CHRIST'S invitation to love God with all our heart, soul, mind, and strength is a lifetime adventure. It is a journey that will never end. Every time we think we have reached the limit, we suddenly turn a corner and discover new horizons, new depths in our own being as well as new wonders in the inexhaustible mystery of God. God is infinite, and infinitely loveable. Even after our earthly pilgrimage concludes and we find ourselves—please God—face-to-face with the Lord, loving him will continue to surprise and delight us in new, fresh ways for all eternity.

This is the only adventure that is worth living and dying for. It is the adventure that we were each created to experience. And each one of us will experience it in a unique way—no one else can love God, or discover God's love, the way you can.

It's especially important to recall *both* of those aspects: Our love for God never comes first; it is *always* a response to God's love for us. He is the vine, we are just the branches; as we have seen various times during this book, without him we can do nothing (see John 15:5).

Keeping that in mind is the secret to being a deeply joy-filled Christian, in spite of our many faults and failings, in spite of the twists and turns of the Christian road, and in spite of the reality of evil in this fallen world. By remembering day in and day out that God is the one most interested in our growth in love, and that he does 99 percent of what needs to be done, we can learn to welcome St. Paul's otherwise puzzling exhortation to "rejoice always. Pray without ceasing. In all circumstances give thanks, for this is the will of God for you in Christ Jesus" (1 Thessalonians 5:16–18).

This introductory explanation of how to begin integrating the various sectors of our human nature into our friendship with Christ so we can gradually come to love him totally was not meant to be exhaustive. And it was not meant to provide a connect-the-dots kind of formula for Christian living. Love is too personal and surprising and vital for that kind of thing. But if it has helped you understand a little bit better the common characteristics of the path that every disciple of Christ must somehow follow, and if it has stirred up or reinforced your desire to keep following that path, and if it has provided one or two (or maybe even three) new insights or suggestions that will help you turn that desire into day-to-day decisions that give glory to the Lord and overflow in love, then we can both be grateful to God, the giver of every good gift.

APPENDIX
Suggestions for Further Reading, Prayer, and Study

Chapter 1: How Much Is Up to Me?

CCC (*Catechism of the Catholic Church*), 348 on responding to the will of God; 153–155 on faith as both a grace and a human act; 2062–2063 on the moral life as a free response to God's loving initiative

I Believe in Love, by Fr. Jean C. J. D'Elbée (Sophia Institute Press, 2001)

Chapter 2: God Is Faithful

CCC, 214–221 on God's primary characteristics of truth and love; 222–227 on the practical consequences of believing in one, faithful, all-powerful God; 1061–1065 on the meaning of "Amen"

The Life of Faustina Kowalksa: The Authorized Biography, by Sister Sophia Michalenko (Servant Books, 1999)

Chapter 3: Spiritual Combat

CCC, 407–409 on the hard battle of life in a fallen world; 391–395 on the devil and the other fallen angels; 1730–1742 on human freedom and salvation

Navigating the Interior Life, by Daniel Burke (Emmaus Road Publishing, 2012)

Chapter 4: Good Soil

CCC, 1810–1811 on the relationship between human virtue and divine grace; 1996–2003 on the mysterious action of God's grace; 166–167 on faith as a personal act in response to God's initiative

Introduction to the Devout Life, by St. Francis de Sales (Tan Books, 1994)

Chapter 5: Full Freedom

CCC, 1, 25, 45 on the primacy of God's love for our spiritual growth; 1700 for a definitive affirmation of the partnership between God and man in the pursuit of spiritual maturity; 1720–1724 on the Christian understanding of happiness

In the School of the Holy Spirit, by Fr. Jacques Philippe (Scepter Books, 2010)

Chapter 6: Loving with My All

CCC, 2083 on the love of God being the source of our response of love; 547–549 on how the deeds of Jesus relate to the message of Jesus; 278 on the reality of God's love; 2560 on God's desire for us to desire him

The Imitation of Christ, by Thomas à Kempis (Catholic Book Publishing, 1985)

Chapter 7: Focusing on the Heart

CCC, 2729 on how to discover interior attachments that inhibit us from loving God with all our heart; 2742 on the relationship between love and prayer

The Story of a Soul, by St. Thérèse of Lisieux (ICS Publications, 1996)

Chapter 8: My Deepest Desire

CCC, 2534–2557 on the relationship between poverty of spirit, desires, and loving God

He Leadeth Me, by Fr. Walter Ciszek, SJ (Ignatius Press, 1995)

Chapter 9: Nourishing My Heart

CCC, 2700–2719 on the different forms of prayer; 1391–1401 on the benefits of receiving the Eucharist; 1468–1470 on the effects of the sacrament of confession

A Handbook of Spiritual Perfection, by Fr. Philip E. Dion (Sophia Institute Press, 2001)

Chapter 10: Freeing My Heart

CCC, 2052–2074 on the Ten Commandments in general; 1849–1851 on the nature of sin

Heroes of God, by Henri Daniel-Rops (Sophia Institute Press, 2002)

Chapter 11: Weak but Wonderful

CCC, 355–379 on the Christian vision of the human person; 1701–1709 on the human person being created in the image of God

Confessions, by St. Augustine (various editions available)

Chapter 12: Understanding Emotions

CCC, 1762–1775 on the role of emotions in human experience; 456–478 on Jesus's complete human nature

The Logic of Desire: Aquinas on Emotion, by Nicholas E. Lombardo (Catholic University of America Press, 2010)

Chapter 13: Emotions in a Fallen World

CCC, 908 on healthy self-mastery; 1804, 1809 on how virtues relate to emotions; 1792 on the danger of being enslaved to one's passions

Searching for and Maintaining Peace: A Small Treatise on Peace of Heart, Fr. Jacques Philippe (Alba House, 2002)

Chapter 14: Forming My Emotions

CCC, 362–368 on the unity of the human person, body and soul; 1803–1821 on the human and theological virtues

Life Up Your Heart: A Guide to Spiritual Peace, by Archbishop Fulton J. Sheen (Ligouri, 1997)

Chapter 15: Following the Light

CCC, 402–406 on the consequences of original sin for human nature; 51–73 on various essential aspects of God's revelation

Theology and Sanity, by Frank Sheed (Ignatius Press, 1993)

Chapter 16: Where to Seek the Truth

CCC, 4–25 on handing on the faith and the basic structure of the Catholic *Catechism*; 74–100 on the Magisterium and the Church's heritage of faith; 751–780 on the origin and mystery of the Church

A Map of Life, by Frank Sheed (Ignatius Press, 1994)

Chapter 17: More Than Information

CCC, 1950–1974 on the relationship between God's wisdom and the moral law; 2651 on the relationship between prayer and study

This Tremendous Lover, by M. Eugene Boylan (Ave Maria, 2009)

Chapter 18: Leveraging the Power of Literature and Art

CCC, 2500–2503, 2513 on truth, beauty, and sacred art; 2493–2499 on mass media

The Return of the Prodigal Son: A Story of Homecoming, by Henry Nouwen (Image Books, 1994)

Chapter 19: Spiritual Gluttony

CCC, 1846–1876 on the nature and proliferation of sin; on the relationship between God's wisdom and the moral law; 282–289 on the importance of catechesis about creation, as an example of an important intersection between faith and reason, where both prayer and study are necessary elements

Time Management for Catholics, by Dave Durand (Crossroad Publishing Company, second edition 2012)

Chapter 20: The Strength to Decide

CCC, 1730–1748 on the Christian understanding of human freedom, its relation to human dignity, and threats against it

Saintly Solutions to Life's Common Problems: From Anger, Boredom, and

Temptation to Gluttony, Gossip, and Greed, by Joseph M. Esper (Sophia Institute Press, 2001)

Chapter 21: Building Well

CCC, 1701–1715 on human nature as the image of God, and on how grace restores what sin has damaged in that human nature

The Art of Loving God, St. Francis de Sales

Chapter 22: Persevering

CCC, 1247–1249 on moving toward maturity in the faith; 1285–1301 on the sacrament of confirmation as the completion of Christian initiation and a sign of spiritual maturity

Three Philosophies of Life, by Peter Kreeft (Ignatius Press, 2009)

Chapter 23: This Present Darkness

CCC, 407–409 on mankind's struggle against the powers of darkness; 538–540 on Jesus and the temptations in the desert; 2846–2854 on temptation and the powers of evil

The Screwtape Letters, by C. S. Lewis (various editions available)

Chapter 24: The Path of Life

CCC, 45, 1057, 1720–1724, 2534–2557, 1817–1821 on the Christian understanding of happiness

Forget Not Love: The Passion of Maximilian Kolbe, by André Frossard (Ignatius Press, 1991)

Chapter 25: A Profile of Virtue

CCC, 1803–1845 on the virtues and their relationship to God's grace

Back to Virtue: Traditional Moral Wisdom for Modern Moral Confusion, by Peter Kreeft (Ignatius Press, 1992)

Chapter 26: Exercising the Virtues

CCC, 2725–2745 on the life of prayer; 2168–2195 on living the Lord's Day as the Lord wills

The Better Part: A Christ-Centered Resource for Personal Prayer, by John Bartunek, LC, STD (Catholic Spiritual Direction, 2011)

Chapter 27: Spiritual Input

CCC, 2514–2557 on the ninth and tenth commandments, which have to do with where we direct our thoughts and the attention of our hearts

Lessons from the Lives of the Saints: A Daily Guide for Growth in Holiness, by Fr. Joseph Esper (Basilica Press, 1999)

Chapter 28: Spiritual Allies

CCC, 1076 on the nature of the Church's liturgical life; 2197–2257 on the Christian vision of family life; 2347 on the value of friendship; 1939–1942 on human solidarity

Surprised by Truth, ed. Patrick Madrid (Sophia Institute Press, any of the multiple volumes)

Chapter 29: Hungering for God's Will

CCC, 2822–2827 on the meaning and importance of seeking and fulfilling God's will; 1786–1789 on moral decisions and the will of God

Discerning the Will of God: An Ignatian Guide to Christian Decision Making, by Timothy M. Gallagher, OMV (Crossroad Publishing Company, 2009)

Chapter 30: Taking Up the Cross

CCC, 309–314 on the problem of evil; 599–623 on the meaning of Christ's self-sacrifice on the cross and how we participate in that sacrifice through our own crosses

The Fulfillment of All Desire, by Ralph Martin (Emmaus Road, 2006)

Acknowledgments

This book would not have been possible without the collaboration of a vast team of fellow pilgrims, especially the following, whom I want to thank sincerely: Cecilia Azcunaga, Lisa Brenninkmeyer, Daniel Burke, Luly Fernandez, Debra Graspointner, Lucy Honner, Fr. Owen Kearns, Paul McCusker, Jennifer Meyer, Fr. Dermot Ryan, Alli Shoemaker, Michele Sylvestro, Doug Venne, DJ Venne, Claudia Volkman, Mike Williams, and the Atlanta, Georgia, community of Consecrated Women of Regnum Christi.

More Titles from Father John Bartunek

Retreat Guide Series

A Guide to Christian Mediation: How to Engage in Personal Prayer

The Better Part: A Christ-Centered Resource for Personal Prayer